THE BEDFORD SERIES IN HISTORY AND CULTURE

The Public Art of
Civil War Commemoration

A Brief History with Documents

Related Titles in
THE BEDFORD SERIES IN HISTORY AND CULTURE
Advisory Editors: Lynn Hunt, *University of California, Los Angeles*
David W. Blight, *Yale University*
Bonnie G. Smith, *Rutgers University*
Natalie Zemon Davis, *Princeton University*
Ernest R. May, *Harvard University*

THE BEDFORD SERIES IN HISTORY AND CULTURE

The Public Art of Civil War Commemoration

A Brief History with Documents

Thomas J. Brown

University of South Carolina

BEDFORD/ST. MARTIN'S   Boston ♦ New York

For Bedford/St. Martin's

Publisher for History: Patricia A. Rossi
Director of Development for History: Jane Knetzger
Developmental Editor: Sara Wise
Editorial Assistant: Carina Schoenberger
Assistant Editor, Publishing Services: Maria Burwell
Senior Production Supervisor: Dennis J. Conroy
Production Associate: Christie Gross
Senior Marketing Manager: Jenna Bookin Barry
Project Management: Books By Design, Inc.
Text Design: Claire Seng-Niemoeller
Indexer: Books By Design, Inc.
Cover Design: Billy Boardman
Cover Photo: The Roxbury Soldiers Monument at Forest Hills Cemetery in Jamaica Plain, Massachusetts. © Richard Heath
Composition: Stratford Publishing Services, Inc.
Printing and Binding: Haddon Craftsmen, an RR Donnelley & Sons Company

President: Joan E. Feinberg
Editorial Director: Denise B. Wydra
Director of Marketing: Karen Melton Soeltz
Director of Editing, Design, and Production: Marcia Cohen
Manager, Publishing Services: Emily Berleth

Library of Congress Control Number: 2003111545

Manufactured in the United States of America.

9 8 7 6
f e d c

For information, write: Bedford/St. Martin's, 75 Arlington Street, Boston, MA 02116 (617-399-4000)

ISBN-10: 0-312-39791-7
ISBN-13: 978-0-312-39791-3

Acknowledgments

Acknowledgments and copyrights appear at the back of the book on page 180, which constitutes an extension of the copyright page.

Foreword

The Bedford Series in History and Culture is designed so that readers can study the past as historians do.

The historian's first task is finding the evidence. Documents, letters, memoirs, interviews, pictures, movies, novels, or poems can provide facts and clues. Then the historian questions and compares the sources. There is more to do than in a courtroom, for hearsay evidence is welcome, and the historian is usually looking for answers beyond act and motive. Different views of an event may be as important as a single verdict. How a story is told may yield as much information as what it says.

Along the way the historian seeks help from other historians and perhaps from specialists in other disciplines. Finally, it is time to write, to decide on an interpretation and how to arrange the evidence for readers.

Each book in this series contains an important historical document or group of documents, each document a witness from the past and open to interpretation in different ways. The documents are combined with some element of historical narrative—an introduction or a biographical essay, for example—that provides students with an analysis of the primary source material and important background information about the world in which it was produced.

Each book in the series focuses on a specific topic within a specific historical period. Each provides a basis for lively thought and discussion about several aspects of the topic and the historian's role. Each is short enough (and inexpensive enough) to be a reasonable one-week assignment in a college course. Whether as classroom or personal reading, each book in the series provides firsthand experience of the challenge—and fun—of discovering, recreating, and interpreting the past.

Lynn Hunt
David W. Blight
Bonnie G. Smith
Natalie Zemon Davis
Ernest R. May

Preface

In the United States, commemoration of the Civil War has inspired singular energy and purposefulness. Even before the war ended in 1865, Americans struggled over how to memorialize the convulsive experience. Since then, remembrance of the watershed era has produced a vast set of monuments, speeches, poems, reenactments, motion pictures, and other works. In this commemoration Americans have created a kind of public art that addresses issues of nationhood, race relations, gender roles, and cultural continuity in times of social upheaval.

From the Gettysburg Address to the present day, individuals and groups have used commemoration to tell stories of the Civil War that have clashed, combined, and changed. Such stories speak of the Civil War, but they also reveal something of the period and place in which they are told. Recent debates over the display of the Confederate battle flag provide just one example of commemoration that calls for examination of the present as well as the past. Indeed, to examine the public art that commemorates the Civil War is not only to understand a single historical event or to explore American memory; it is also to recognize issues that continue to play a dynamic role in our society. Understanding how the story of the Civil War has been told and retold, often with different emphases and different goals, sheds light on the issues and ideas that have affected American culture for the better part of a century and a half.

This collection of primary texts and illustrations allows readers to analyze some of these narratives and examine how they have shifted over time. A brief introduction outlines the major phases of Civil War commemoration. It describes the most influential forms of shared memory, from the golden age of oratory to the era of electronic communications, and it sketches the leading themes expressed in remembrance of the Civil War. The introduction especially urges students to consider the ways in which different northerners and southerners addressed sectional reunion as a hallmark of national identity, bearing in mind the implications of the reunion motif for divisions of race, class, and gender and for defining the legacy of Confederate defeat.

Following the introduction, five case studies—focused on the commemoration of citizen-soldiers, women of the war, Robert E. Lee, the 54th Massachusetts Infantry Regiment, and Abraham Lincoln—use rich visual and textual sources to illuminate relations among social groups and contests over values. The illustrations are among the most important documents in the book, which seeks not to weigh their artistic merits but to enable students to practice seeing works of art as historical evidence. Each image is discussed at length within the narrative, and all captions contain a thought-provoking question to help students analyze the art. Headnotes to the textual sources similarly provide specific background material for each document and suggest starting points for interpretation. The chronology of Civil War commemoration, questions for consideration, and bibliography that follow the documents provide tools to serve as a basis for informed discussion or further study of the issues that these sources emphasize.

ACKNOWLEDGMENTS

I have compiled many more debts than documents in assembling this book. David Blight's support for the project has been a typical example of his great kindness. Chuck Christensen, Patricia Rossi, Sara Wise, Jessica Angell, and Carina Schoenberger guided this unconventional addition to the Bedford Series in History and Culture with a wonderful combination of patience and enthusiasm. Many thanks to Emily Berleth, Dennis Conroy, Christie Gross, and Nancy Benjamin for their help producing the book. At the University of South Carolina, a College of Liberal Arts Scholarship Support grant helped to fund this venture, and Bob Ellis capably and cheerfully assisted in many ways. Gaines Foster at Louisiana State University, Paul Harvey at University of Colorado at Colorado Springs, Robert May at Purdue University, Kirk Savage at University of Pittsburgh, Nina Silber at Boston

University, Joan Waugh at University of California at Los Angeles, and an anonymous referee offered thoughtful suggestions after reading the manuscript. I am similarly grateful for the aid and encouragement provided at various stages by Elizabeth Barrett, Marty Blatt, Fitz Brundage, John Coski, Walter Edgar, Alice Fahs, William Gienapp, Harry Lesesne, Jim Percoco, Ted Phillips, Michael Vorenberg, Paul Wright, Donald Yacovone, and Elizabeth Young.

If this classroom volume reflects any familiarity with effective pedagogical methods, the credit belongs to the students on whom I have tried out these materials and the outstanding teachers with whom I had the good fortune to study. Lucian and Veronica Brown provided candid daily reminders of students' perspectives on schoolwork. Josie Brown generously let our children think that my part of the process was also work, although she knew full well that for me it was pure fun.

Thomas J. Brown

Contents

Illustrations

The Public Art of Civil War Commemoration

A Brief History with Documents

Introduction:
American Commemoration
and the Civil War

When Abraham Lincoln took the oath of office on March 4, 1861, he faced a situation that challenged him to explain what held the United States together. Seven slaveholding states had seceded from the Union in direct response to his election, and it was possible that others might follow suit. Lincoln's inaugural address restated his commitment to the permanence of the Union. After discussing the constitutional basis for his position and alluding to the practical benefits of unity, he devoted his closing lines to his most fervent appeal to Americans to remain true to their common country:

> Though passion may have strained, it must not break our bonds of affection. The mystic chords of memory, stretching from every battle-field, and patriot grave, to every living heart and hearthstone, all over this broad land, will yet swell the chorus of the Union, when again touched, as surely they will be, by the better angels of our nature.

Lincoln's reliance on "the mystic chords of memory" as a basis of collective identity reflected an important trend. In the aftermath of the American Revolution the new nation had established a commemorative ritual on July 4 and identified a central hero in George Washington, but only long after independence did historical consciousness become a defining element of American culture. The acclaim for Daniel Webster's orations on the bicentennial anniversary of the Pilgrims' landing at Plymouth (1820) and the cornerstone-laying for the Bunker Hill monument (1825) marked a growing interest in commemoration nourished by romanticism and the expansion of participatory democracy. The first large-scale historic preservation campaign in

United States history, an attempt to ensure the survival of Washington's home at Mount Vernon, illustrated the political uses of remembrance that became widespread by the 1850s. To raise funds for the preservation campaign, and use it as a rallying point for Unionism amid the deepening sectional crisis, Massachusetts statesman and orator Edward Everett delivered his speech on Washington's life more than 135 times across the country. Lincoln's inaugural invocation of "every battle-field and patriot grave" similarly suggested that symbolically important sites radiated a collective memory reaching to "every living heart and hearthstone."[1]

The retrospective impulse influenced the ways in which the Union and Confederacy sought to mobilize support for the war. Both sides presented their cause as the continuation of American history. The Confederate national seal depicted the equestrian statue of Washington dedicated in Richmond three years before the outbreak of the war, and Jefferson Davis took the oath of office as the first president under the permanent Confederate constitution on Washington's birthday in 1862. Union general Benjamin F. Butler demonstrated the shared eagerness to construct a usable past when he ordered the equestrian statue of Andrew Jackson in occupied New Orleans inscribed "The Union Must and Shall Be Preserved." Of course, the events of the war provided rich new material for remembrance on both sides.

The expansion of American commemoration continued to accelerate after the Civil War. The celebration of the centennial of the American Revolution, highlighted by the Philadelphia Exposition of 1876, dwarfed the semicentennial observances and set the pace for a variety of anniversary spectacles in cities across the country. Lineage-based groups like the Daughters of the American Revolution, the Colonial Dames of America, and the Society of Mayflower Descendants proliferated in the 1890s. Historic preservation campaigns intensified and began to coalesce in such organizations as the Association for the Preservation of Virginia Antiquities (1889) and the American Scenic and Historic Preservation Society (1895).[2]

Remembrance of the Civil War held a special position in this developing culture of memory. The deaths of approximately 620,000 soldiers claimed the thoughts of families throughout the North and South. Millions of Americans regarded the war as the most momentous period of their lives. A few years before Walt Whitman died in

1892, a friend asked the poet if he ever went back to those days; Whitman replied, "I have never left them."[3] Commemoration drew energy from, and supplied direction to, the enormous investment of individuals in recalling the war and finding lessons in it. And while many different kinds of shared memory constituted political capital, the Civil War was the indispensable reference point for the leading public issues of postwar society. In an age when commemoration of the colonial and Revolutionary periods was helping to fix national attention on the past, remembrance of the Civil War pervaded American life.

At the same time that it responded to immediate psychological and political pressures, Civil War commemoration established a long-term framework for fashioning personal and collective identity in the United States. Robert Penn Warren declared in 1961 that "the Civil War is our only 'felt' history—history lived in the national imagination."[4] As Warren hastened to add, Americans have differed sharply in the way they have imagined the war. They have focused on a wide range of stories in its overarching narrative, and they have told the same stories from many perspectives. But the intensity of remembrance has made the Civil War a mythic construction in which generations of Americans have found models for leading individual lives and a drama infusing life into the entity of the nation.

PHASES OF CIVIL WAR COMMEMORATION

This book presents five case studies in Civil War remembrance, examining tributes to the citizen-soldier, women of the war, Robert E. Lee, the 54th Massachusetts Infantry Regiment, and Abraham Lincoln. Each chapter traces the development of commemoration from the war years to the present. These trajectories are partly distinctive to the separate topics, but they also reflect broader patterns of periodization defined by shifts in the apparatus that has produced Civil War memory as well as shifts in the ideas that Americans have found compelling in their recollections of the war.

The links between sponsorship and content in commemoration were particularly evident in the efforts of political parties to tap Civil War memory during the generation after Appomattox. Even as they moved away from the focus on issues of slavery and freedom that had given birth to the party, Republicans were quick to remind voters that they had led the successful defense of the Union, a strategy that Democrats labeled "waving the bloody shirt." And well after that theme faded, Republicans sought to enhance and benefit from the popularity of Lincoln. Southern Democrats in turn relied heavily on their identification with the Confederacy. Rebel veterans comprised more than 70 percent of the members of the Forty-Fifth Congress (1877–1879) from the former Confederate states and almost 50 percent of the southern delegation as late as the Fifty-Fourth Congress (1895–1897).[5]

Veterans' groups initially formed to combine partisanship with remembrance of the ordeal of warfare. The Ku Klux Klan, established by former Confederate soldiers in Pulaski, Tennessee, in 1866, perpetrated extralegal political violence in hooded costumes intended to identify Klan members with the ghosts of fallen comrades. The Grand Army of the Republic (GAR), a society for Union veterans founded in Decatur, Illinois, in April 1866, did not share the sinister aspects of the Klan, but it also recalled the traumatic experiences of front-line troops and dedicated itself to political action, rallying behind the leadership of former Union general John A. Logan. In the 1880s, however, the GAR developed into a fraternal organization with a broader membership and a less partisan ideological agenda. By 1890, the organization boasted more than 350,000 members in local posts around the country, over one-third of the surviving Union veterans. The counterpart United Confederate Veterans (UCV) formed in 1889. Fifteen years later, it claimed 1,565 local camps and a total membership of approximately 80,000, estimated to be between one-third and one-fourth of surviving Confederate veterans. Many of the Civil War armies and regiments also had active alumni societies. These organizations faded away as the ex-soldiers died, although the UCV fostered the formation in 1896 of a successor organization, the Sons of Confederate Veterans (SCV), which had 16,000 members in 1903.[6]

The evolution of women's commemorative groups similarly illustrated the late-nineteenth-century shift in the Civil War memory. Ladies Memorial Associations formed in communities throughout the South shortly after the war to attend to the final disposition of soldiers' remains and sponsor mourning ceremonies and monuments. The establishment of the United Daughters of the Confederacy (UDC) in 1894 created an organizational structure beyond the local level and sustained commemoration as an everyday social activity rather than a series of isolated projects like reinterments or annual Memorial Day observances. The UDC grew rapidly to include 138 local chapters within three years and almost 100,000 members by World War I. Its northern counterpart was the Women's Relief Corps (WRC), which formed in 1883 when the GAR invited a Massachusetts coalition of veterans aid societies to create a national commemorative body. The group numbered more than 100,000 members from 1892 to 1919.[7]

Popular magazines demonstrate the expansion of the market for Civil War remembrance in the 1880s. After responding to the intense national absorption in the war as it unfolded, publishers had retreated somewhat from the topic during the 1870s. *Harper's Weekly* and *Harper's Monthly,* which published more than two hundred short stories about the war by 1865, largely stopped carrying war fiction.[8] A revival blossomed with the appearance of a series of war reminiscences in *Century* magazine from November 1884 to November 1887 that helped to increase circulation from 127,000 to 225,000 in the first six months and provided the basis for a successful four-volume collection of memoirs, *Battles and Leaders of the Civil War* (1888).[9] The reinvigorated reading market for Civil War memory was even sufficient to support magazines devoted exclusively to it. *Confederate Veteran* (1893–1932) boasted a peak circulation of 20,000 at the turn of the century.[10] Popular magazines, moreover, were only one example of the convergence between remembrance and entrepreneurship. Railroads and merchants encouraged veterans' reunions, the development of battlefield parks shared in the growth of the tourism industry, and printmakers sought to stimulate consumer demand for images associated with the war.

This book devotes special attention to public monuments, a cultural form that was at the peak of its popularity in the period from the 1850s through the phase of Civil War commemoration that began in the 1880s. The war was by far the most frequently represented historical subject in the thousands of monuments Americans dedicated before the form fell from favor during the 1920s. These works frequently served as focal points for contests over memory of the war, for the construction of a monument is a political process that routinely requires sponsors to obtain public space, agree on a design, and raise funds. Like other political processes, memorial projects have reflected the distribution of power within the United States. Monuments often purport to stand for the shared views of a community that in fact is divided, and in that sense they offer only a limited record of American memory of the Civil War. But memorials are not merely permanent images of temporarily dominant viewpoints; they are sites of negotiation among different ideological positions, both within the sponsoring group and outside of it. Those negotiations have often continued well after the dedication ceremony, for the monument is a product not only of the period in which it was installed but also of the constantly changing civic landscape. Its meaning may be adjusted by ceremonies held at the site, embellishment of the surrounding area, or literary depictions. At once the most solidly fixed and the most open-ended form of remembrance, the public monument connects Civil War commemoration in the past and the present.

The decline in the commissioning of public monuments during the 1920s partly reflected technological innovations that affected the mechanisms of Civil War remembrance. Monuments tended to be obstacles for rapidly proliferating automobiles, which gave rise to new forms of commemoration like highways named for Abraham Lincoln, Robert E. Lee, and Jefferson Davis. Even more significant for American memory was the rise of the motion picture industry. Such films as *Birth of a Nation* (1915), *Gone With the Wind* (1939), *Young Mr. Lincoln* (1939), and *Abe Lincoln in Illinois* (1940) in some ways assumed the cultural role of the public monument. The movies, however, did so in a very different form that reshaped commemoration at the same time that the intellectual attitudes of the World War I era were challenging the Victorian context of previous Civil War remembrance.

The most recent phase of Civil War commemoration has similarly been characterized both by its leading themes, most notably the focus on race relations intensified by the civil rights movement of the 1950s and 1960s, and by the emergence of new forms. In some cases these innovations were again technological. The spread of television would demonstrate its full commemorative potential when the first episode of Ken Burns's documentary series *The Civil War* (1990) attracted an estimated 13.9 million viewers.[11] But other vehicles of memory also developed influence during the same period, most notably the practice of "re-enacting" military encampments and engagements of the war. Contemporary remembrance of the Civil War, like commemoration during and immediately after the war, or in the phases that began around 1880 and 1920, provides an excellent opportunity to examine the relationships between the productive apparatus and the content of American culture.

MAJOR THEMES OF CIVIL WAR COMMEMORATION

The most prominent motif in early Civil War commemoration was the theme that Lincoln anticipated in his appeal to "the mystic chords of memory." It was not a coincidence that Lincoln emphasized antebellum American memory at battlefields and patriot graves, but northern and southern remembrance of the Civil War would concentrate much more heavily on the experiences and sacrifices of soldiers. Commemoration of the Revolutionary War offers a useful point of comparison, for memory of the Minutemen and Valley Forge was balanced by the political anniversary on July 4 and a constellation of celebrated noncombatants like Patrick Henry and Paul Revere. In contrast, after the Civil War even the commemoration of Lincoln owed a good deal to the martyrdom he shared with fallen soldiers.

If the staggering death toll in the Civil War was the most obvious reason for the cultural power of its battlefields and patriot graves, public commemoration in the North turned to the idea of the nation as the primary response to this experience of loss. Lincoln's first inaugural address had marked out a standard formula in suggesting that the dead lived on in memories that constituted the United States. He would return to that theme in much greater depth and significantly different terms at Gettysburg, and countless other speakers would join him in adapting religious narratives of death and rebirth. The sequence applied not only to the national life that followed individual deaths but also to the figurative death and rebirth of the country itself in the transformation from division to reunion, as Americans embraced poet William Butler Yeats's observation that "nothing can be sole or whole / That has not been rent."

This framework left significant room for debate over the terms of the national regeneration. Within that contested space, the clearest shift in northern commemoration from the 1860s to the early twentieth century was an increased tendency to look favorably on the Confederacy. This view of the war matched a more general pattern in the changing image of the South. Before the war, conservative northerners had often portrayed the South as an orderly pastoral counterpart to the materialism and social fluidity of the rapidly developing North. The ideological perspective maturing with the Republican party challenged that romanticization and stressed the failure of democracy and the degradation of labor that even northern conservatives identified as impediments to progress in the South. During the decades after the war, northern literature and tourism practices reconstructed the image of the South as a place of respite from the economic and social pressures of life in the North. The North provided a strong market for the sentimental picture of the Old South popularized by late-nineteenth-century southern writers like Thomas Nelson Page and Joel Chandler Harris, and northern authors further embellished idealization of the region through such works as Owen Wister's bestselling novel *The Virginian* (1902), which welded the appeal of the South and the West to create an influential portrait of the American cowboy.[12]

Increased northern admiration for the South expressed itself in Civil War commemoration primarily through attitudes toward Confederate soldiers. The image of Robert E. Lee is a leading example of this process, but views of rank-and-file soldiers followed a similar path. Condemnation of Confederate troops as the traitorous pawns of slaveholders had faded considerably by the simultaneous end of political Reconstruction and celebration of the Revolutionary centennial. General Francis Bartlett of Massachusetts received wide praise for declaring at the 1875 anniversary of the battles of Lexington and Concord that "as an American, I am as proud of the men who charged so bravely with Pickett's division on our lines at Gettysburg, as I am of the men who so bravely met and repulsed them there."[13] A series of intersectional Blue-Gray veterans' reunions in the 1880s reinforced this sentiment. Highly publicized festivities accompanied the 1895 dedication of a Chicago monument that recognized Confederate soldiers who had died in the city as prisoners of war, and in 1900 a section for Confederate dead was set aside at Arlington National Cemetery.

This shift did not go unchallenged. African Americans and their allies resisted the advance in northern deference to Confederate soldiers that accompanied a retreat from northern protection of black rights codified in Reconstruction. Frederick Douglass stressed that the Civil War "was not a mere display of brute courage and endurance, but it was a war between men of thought as well as of action, and in dead earnest for something beyond the battlefield."[14] Regardless of their racial views, Union veterans also expressed ambivalence about the trend. While glad to praise martial virtues and to acknowledge that they had faced a worthy foe, Union veterans opposed any downplaying of their achievements in winning the war and saving the nation. When President Grover Cleveland called in 1887 for a return of captured Confederate battle flags, the Grand Army of the Republic's protests forced him to abandon the proposal. By the twentieth century, however, opposition to northern outreach faded as Union veterans dwindled in number and identified more often with their fellow veterans from the South. Congress voted to return the captured flags in 1905.

The shift in northern remembrance of the Civil War requires explanation. Northern whites' weak commitment to black rights may have been a necessary precondition to the increasing praise for the military merits of Confederate soldiers without regard for the cause they supported, but it is less clear that white supremacism was sufficient to propel northerners into an embrace of their former foes. During the Civil War, white northerners had often combined racism with hatred of the Confederacy.

Many scholars have identified the impetus for the shift of northern memory in a desire, or need, for a national solidity firmer than military triumph could ensure. In the first major study of the topic, Paul Buck declared that "the reunited nation was a fact" only after "the memories of the past were woven in a web of national sentiment which selected from bygone feuds those deeds of mutual valor which permitted pride in present achievement and future promise." This analysis echoed the words of countless Americans from the turn of the century, although the sense in which northerners enjoyed a more reunited nation in 1900 than in 1870 remains somewhat elusive. No prospect existed at either point that southern states would again attempt secession. Nor can successful postwar initiatives easily be attributed to improvements in intersectional cooperation. Buck and others have noted that the Spanish-American War "advertised the fact that the people of the United States were a nation," but white southerners had not resisted the expansionism of William Henry Seward in the 1860s.[15] To be sure, former Confederates often said that they were pleased by northern praise. That approval seems inadequate, however, to explain the energy that a prickly New Englander like Charles Francis Adams Jr. devoted to rehabilitating the Confederate reputation. (See Document 14.)

Reunion might best be regarded as a partly straightforward and partly symbolic theme in Civil War commemoration. As the idea of nationhood increasingly came to be defined in terms of citizens' emotions, rather than laws or institutions, many northerners wished to alleviate the frustration of defeated southerners. At the same time, the reunion motif offered a way to address other issues. It celebrated the integrity of the United States at a time when many northerners worried that the influx of immigration imperiled American identity. The concept of reunion also served as a broader metaphorical response to anxieties about social fragmentation. Historian Nina Silber has pointed out that representations of the North-South reunion as a marriage not only idealized political bonds but lent the prestige of nationalism to the institution of marriage during a period of declining marriage rates and rising divorce rates. Class divisions loomed even more ominously for the business and social elites who led the creation of what Silber calls the northern "culture of conciliation."[16] Civil War remembrance is a flexible language, and careful reading is necessary to determine its meanings in particular situations.

Postwar white southern commemoration of the Confederacy, often called the cult of "the Lost Cause," overlapped in some ways with the ideology of sectional reconciliation but also involved a distinct set of issues. Unlike Union tributes, remembrance of the Confederacy could not justify the sacrifices on its behalf by pointing to the permanence of the nation. White southerners who had maintained that their cause implemented God's plan for humanity were compelled to explain the apparent evidence of divine disfavor. Promotion of the soldier as a model of masculinity and citizenship in postwar society faced the obstacle that Confederate soldiers had failed.

White southern remembrance represented a complicated negotiation of these points. Unlike shared memory of unsuccessful rebellions in Ireland or Poland, Confederate commemoration did not become a rallying point for renewed commitment to independence. White southerners often declared that they were glad secession had failed, and southern nationalist ideologues like Edmund Ruffin, who committed suicide in 1865 rather than live in a reunified country, found little room in the pantheon of the Lost Cause. On the other hand, many white southerners resisted Reconstruction with tactics that virtually amounted to a continuation of the war in pursuit of a postemancipation form of racial supremacy. Confederate commemoration was important in this struggle, as it had been before Appomattox, though white southerners now abandoned attempts to justify the institution of slavery. They increasingly insisted that the sectional conflict centered not on slavery but on issues of "states' rights," or the extent to which the Constitution entitled state governments to regulate internal affairs without federal supervision.

After the return to so-called home rule, the culture of conciliation and the Lost Cause continued to interact as they coalesced in the late nineteenth century. The celebration of reunion reinforced the notion that the white South had been united in the sectional conflict, when in fact the Confederacy enjoyed far more unanimous support in memory than it had during its tumultuous existence. Kentucky, which supplied the Confederacy with only half as many white soldiers as it contributed to the Union and only about one-third as many total soldiers, dedicated more than forty monuments to Confederate soldiers, three monuments to Union soldiers, and one monument to the soldiers of both sides between 1865 and 1920; another five monuments in national cemeteries typified the regional representation of Unionism as an alien force occupying scattered beachheads in the state. As that landscape pattern suggests, Confederate commemoration created a cultural infrastructure that in some ways became more rather than less strident, despite the culture of conciliation. Confederate veterans' interest in Blue-Gray reunions declined in the South in the 1890s while Union veterans' interest increased. White southerners were also consistently less enthusiastic than white northerners about the virtues of their former foes. While interest in the dedication of a monument to Lee in Washington, D.C., gathered strength in the early twentieth century, an effort by several Confederate veterans to place a monument to Grant in Richmond raised a total of sixteen dollars.[17] Less widespread though noteworthy was the persistence of an even firmer white southern resistance to the ideology of reconciliation that resented the assimilation of Confederate icons like Lee into the repertory of American symbols.

Related to the complexity of reunion in the Lost Cause was the problematic place of defeat in Confederate remembrance. Much white southern commemoration celebrated a triumph that belied the final results from the battlefield. According to this view, Confederate soldiers had worn themselves out whipping the Yankees and had forged a moral example that served as a beacon to the nation and the world. Minister J. J. Taylor declared at the 1906 dedication of a Confederate monument in Shreveport, Louisiana, that "all the great reforms among nations, and all the mighty strides of the people toward constitutional government and personal liberty, have had their genesis and their clearest expressions in the principles for which the Confederate soldier fought and died."[18] While insisting on a distinctive regional achievement, this interpretation envisioned participation in a traditional American parade of progress. As in the North, the terms of that regeneration were vigorously debated. Champions of the New South argued that it should take the form of an industrialization sanctioned by fidelity to the stainless virtue of the Confederate soldier, much to the dismay of white southerners who regarded the ballyhooed New South as the antithesis of the Confederacy.

Triumphalist southern memory has competed with a tragic perspective identifying permanent defeat as the heart of the Confederate legacy. Thomas Connelly and Barbara Bellows have argued that Confederate commemoration contrasted with the basic narratives of United States history because "the Lost Cause was a realization of mortality existing in an America that reached for the gnostic immortal; it was an admission of failure juxtaposed against national faith in success and achievement." For them, the main current of white southern memory expressed "that peculiar classical-Christian mentality that produced a distinct view of the tragedy of the never-changing human condition."[19] William Faulkner, Robert Penn Warren, C. Vann Woodward, and other twentieth-century southern writers made these themes central to their work.

In addition to the distinctive themes it explored in its formative era, commemoration of the Confederacy has charted a unique path of decline. Remembrance of the Union cause has pitted the periodic reinvigoration of selected topics against the broad tendency toward erosion. Remarkable revivals of interest have centered at various times on citizen-soldiers, Lincoln, and the 54th Massachusetts Infantry Regiment, but former heroes like naval commander David Farragut and cavalry leader Philip Sheridan have long since followed previous American idols like Henry Clay by "slipping into the limbo of lost souls, the history books."[20] Remembrance of the Confederacy has similarly involved resurgences within an overall pattern of attenuation; Allen Tate's "Ode to the Confederate Dead," originally written in 1927, tried to catch a moment at which tradition faded from contact with modern life. But commemoration of the Confederacy has also been directly repudiated at times as Americans have grown readier to see through Lost Cause claims that the country divided over "states' rights" and to denounce the Confederate defense of slavery. Communities throughout the South have discussed the renaming of streets and schools and the removal of monuments. When New Orleans decided to change the names of all schools that honored slaveholders, the P. G. T. Beauregard Junior High School became the Thurgood Marshall Middle School.

The exact resolution of this sharply contested process remains unclear, but it marks an important event in the history of American memory. In the years since patriots toppled the equestrian statue of George III in New York City after issuance of the Declaration of Independence, commemoration in the United States has developed mostly through selective renewals and shifts in emphasis rather than open retraction of previous acts of commemoration. While new attitudes toward the Confederacy are only part of the reexamination of the legacy of slavery—and slavery is not the only element of the American past to have prompted calls for repudiation—public remembrance of the Confederacy is the most extensive commemorative infrastructure to have faced such a strong challenge. In so clearly puncturing the illusion of a continuous tradition and energizing debate over the significance of commemoration, memory of the Civil War has again served as an important vehicle for negotiation of American identity.

NOTES

[1]Originally drafted by William Henry Seward, the "mystic chords of memory" passage in effect replied to John C. Calhoun's famous argument during the crisis of 1850 that "the cords which bind these States together in one common Union" were snapping. For Calhoun, the crucial cords were intersectional institutions like churches

and political parties; for Seward and Lincoln, emotionally resonant chords of remembrance defined the nation.

²Michael Kammen, *The Mystic Chords of Memory: The Transformation of Tradition in American Culture* (New York: Alfred A. Knopf, 1991), surveys the development of commemoration.

³Daniel Aaron, *The Unwritten War: American Writers and the Civil War* (New York: Alfred A. Knopf, 1973), 72.

⁴Robert Penn Warren, *The Legacy of the Civil War* (Cambridge, Mass.: Harvard University Press, 1961), 5.

⁵William W. White, *The Confederate Veteran* (Tuscaloosa, Alabama: Confederate Publishing Company, Inc., 1962), 81–82.

⁶Stuart McConnell, *Glorious Contentment: The Grand Army of the Republic, 1865–1900* (Chapel Hill: University of North Carolina Press, 1992), 54; Gaines Foster, *Ghosts of the Confederacy: Defeat, the Lost Cause, and the Emergence of the New South, 1865–1913* (New York: Oxford University Press, 1987), 107, 172.

⁷Karen Lynne Cox, "Women, the Lost Cause, and the New South: The United Daughters of the Confederacy and the Transmission of Confederate Culture, 1894–1919" (Ph.D. dissertation, University of Southern Mississippi, 1997), 48; Cecelia Elizabeth O'Leary, *To Die For: The Paradox of American Patriotism* (Princeton, N.J.: Princeton University Press, 1999), 83, 100.

⁸David W. Blight, *Race and Reunion: The Civil War in American Memory* (Cambridge, Mass.: The Belknap Press of Harvard University Press, 2001), 150.

⁹Ibid., 174–75.

¹⁰Foster, *Ghosts of the Confederacy*, 106.

¹¹Robert Brent Toplin, ed., *Ken Burns's* The Civil War: *Historians Respond* (New York: Oxford University Press, 1996), xv.

¹²See William R. Taylor, *Cavalier and Yankee: The Old South and American National Character* (New York: George Braziller, 1961); Eric Foner, *Free Soil, Free Labor, Free Men: The Ideology of the Republican Party Before the Civil War* (New York: Oxford University Press, 1970); Nina Silber, *The Romance of Reunion: Northerners and the South, 1865–1900* (Chapel Hill: University of North Carolina Press, 1993).

¹³Paul H. Buck, *The Road to Reunion, 1865–1900* (reprint ed.: New York: Vintage Books, 1959; first published 1937), 140.

¹⁴Blight, *Race and Reunion*, 93.

¹⁵Buck, *Road to Reunion*, 310, 318.

¹⁶Silber, *The Romance of Reunion*, 93, 116–17.

¹⁷Kammen, *Mystic Chords of Memory*, 109.

¹⁸Bettie A. C. Emerson, comp., *Historic Southern Monuments: Representative Memorials of the Heroic Dead of the Southern Confederacy* (New York: Neale Publishing Co., 1911), 157.

¹⁹Thomas L. Connelly and Barbara L. Bellows, *God and General Longstreet: The Lost Cause and the Southern Mind* (Baton Rouge: Louisiana State University Press, 1982), 92–93, 108.

²⁰David Donald, "The Folklore Lincoln," in *Lincoln Reconsidered: Essays on the Civil War Era*, 2nd ed. (New York: Vintage Books, 1961), 145.

1

The Citizen-Soldier

Civil War commemoration raised recognition of the common soldier far beyond the status he had previously enjoyed in American memory. The leading organization of Revolutionary War veterans, the Society of the Cincinnati, was open only to officers and their descendants, and the Aztec Club, formed for veterans of the Mexican-American War, similarly restricted its membership to officers. In contrast, Civil War veterans created many organizations for the former rank-and-file, including most prominently the Grand Army of the Republic and the United Confederate Veterans. The pensions and other government benefits provided to Civil War veterans and their families constituted a much more extensive system of financial recognition than previous veterans had received. The institution of Memorial Day made remembrance of fallen Civil War soldiers a part of the national calendar, and military cemeteries, preserved battlefields, and public monuments emerged as places of commemoration.

These tributes helped to establish the Civil War soldier as a touchstone for negotiations among Americans over several issues. Northerners and southerners alike struggled to develop patterns of mourning responsive to the shocking slaughter of the war. The anguish was heightened by the disparity between Victorian notions of an ideal death—a passage to be experienced peacefully at home while surrounded by family members, followed by a funeral and burial in a cemetery that encouraged contemplative visitors—and the awareness that the bodies of countless unidentified men who had died horrifically lay far from home in unmarked trenches. Commemoration sought to give meaning to these deaths and define the relationship between the dead and the living.

The figure of the soldier also provided a model of postwar citizenship. He represented the political posture, the collective responsibilities, and the ideals of personal appearance prescribed by the society that honored him, including its vision of ethnicity. He was particularly emblematic of ideas about masculinity in the wake of the war and amid the social upheavals that followed it.

Ideas about death and citizenship cut across sectional lines, and recognition for the common soldier often served as a common ground on which Civil War commemoration shifted from affirmation of the principles at stake in the conflict to acclaim for the valor displayed by both sides. This tendency was particularly strong in the North, where tributes to Union soldiers gradually faded into a broader admiration for American soldiers. Commemoration of the Confederate rank and file also participated in this process, but the purposes of those soldiers' sacrifices remained a prominent theme. Along with remembrance of southern military and political leaders and women of the homefront, reverence for the Confederate soldier provided a vehicle for postwar reinterpretation of the political significance of the conflict. Well over a century after the Civil War, commemorations defended as tributes to the Confederate soldier would rank among the most controversial aspects of American memory.

FIELDS OF MEMORY: BURIAL GROUNDS AND BATTLEGROUNDS

Cemeteries and preserved battlefields were among the most novel and influential sites for remembrance of the Civil War soldier. The two types of landscapes overlapped in the most famous example of commemoration during the war, the dedication of the soldiers cemetery at Gettysburg, Pennsylvania, on November 19, 1863. After the war, cemeteries and battlefields developed into distinct forms of memory that typically involved different participants and dramatized different aspects of the citizen-soldier.

The grave of the fallen Civil War soldier created a lasting conjunction of memory and place. This ancient process was new to the remembrance of common soldiers, for the dead troops of previous wars were generally buried in unmarked mass graves. The Civil War saw the emergence of military cemeteries that consisted, as much as possible, of individually marked graves. Established by Congress in July 1862, the federal system included seventy-three cemeteries by

1870; 58 percent of the approximately 300,000 bodies were identified.[1] In the South, private initiatives, particularly by ladies memorial associations, were central to the postwar development of Confederate battlefield cemeteries, and soldiers sections in civilian cemeteries. Although incomplete records made it more difficult to identify the Confederate dead individually, imposing monuments like the ninety-foot-tall granite pyramid placed above the remains of 18,500 troops at Hollywood Cemetery in Richmond testified to the respect for the soldiers' final resting place.

The new institution promoted new ideas about the citizen-soldier. The military cemetery highlighted the sacrifices of the soldier and expressed his relationship to society in spatial terms. In contrast to the scattered or unmarked graves of previous soldiers, the burial places of Civil War soldiers became civic shrines. Memory of the war entered into community life through the experiences of individual cemetery visitors and through such social rituals as funerals, monument dedications, and, especially, Memorial Day. Consistent with designs of the antebellum rural cemetery movement, which presented death as a return to Christian nature and offered a retreat in which the living might reflect, the Civil War cemetery encouraged visitors to admire the soldier's devotion to his cause and examine their own commitments.

The establishment of military cemeteries at or near Civil War battlefields was only one way in which the treatment of these sites differed from the models provided by Revolutionary War battlefields, which had been adorned, if at all, only by an obelisk, usually much more modest than the monument at Bunker Hill. Another important trend was the placement of markers to record and help visitors picture the combat that had taken place on the site. After the installation of several monuments to fallen soldiers at Gettysburg, veterans of the 2nd Massachusetts Regiment installed a memorial in 1879 that marked a position the unit had held during the engagement. By the twenty-fifth anniversary of the battle in 1888, more than 300 monuments filled the field, most of which also illustrated battle lines and honored both veterans and the dead. A campaign launched in the same year culminated in 1890 in legislation establishing the Chickamauga and Chattanooga National Military Park in Georgia and Tennessee. Over the next several years Congress created similar parks at

Shiloh, Tennessee; Gettysburg, Pennsylvania; Vicksburg, Mississippi; and Antietam, Maryland. The federal government provided funds for land acquisition and maintenance, and state governments generally paid for the monuments placed in the parks. Details of development differed at each site, but the presentation of the Civil War battlefields was much more carefully orchestrated than the casual approach that had prevailed at most Revolutionary War battlefields.

Veterans dominated the construction of battlefield parks. They played key roles in the administration of the parks and the state commissions that funded monuments. Park ceremonies, such as dedications of monuments or observance of battle anniversaries, centered on the attendance of veterans. The battlefield parks accordingly reflected veterans' remembrances of the war. Despite hesitation from former Union soldiers who stressed the unique importance of their triumph and from ex-Confederates dissatisfied with a park system initially concentrated on sites of Union victories, the battlefield park provided a key forum for remembrance of the war as a series of military movements, rather than a political conflict, and for celebration of the valor of troops on both sides. Several battlefield monuments would depict Union and Confederate soldiers embracing, a tribute to the sentiments that the parks claimed to have promoted.

Like the soldiers cemetery, the battlefield park established a theater in which different, possibly conflicting, memories of the war might be presented. The continued development of the appearance of the sites and the commemorative events staged in them would do much to determine which themes established the closest associations with these places of memory.

1

ABRAHAM LINCOLN

Gettysburg Address

November 19, 1863

Lincoln (1809–1865) rarely left Washington during the war, but he accepted an invitation shortly before the dedication of the Gettysburg cemetery to make "a few appropriate remarks" after the main oration by Edward Everett. Lincoln organized his speech around a series of juxtapositions. At the center were the connections he wove between the lives of individuals and the life of the nation, a theme climaxing in the "new birth of freedom" to which he called upon his listeners to dedicate themselves. The taut composition envisioned the United States both as the implementation of a set of universal political ideas and as an organic body shaped by unique historical experiences, two conceptions of nationhood that have often competed in American history. It is often noted that Lincoln did not refer to the victory won by the Union army or to the opposing side or to any details of the battle. What are the key words in his address?

Four score and seven years ago our fathers brought forth on this continent, a new nation, conceived in Liberty, and dedicated to the proposition that all men are created equal.

Now we are engaged in a great civil war, testing whether that nation, or any nation so conceived and so dedicated, can long endure. We are met on a great battle-field of that war. We have come to dedicate a portion of that field, as a final resting place for those who here gave their lives that that nation might live. It is altogether fitting and proper that we should do this.

But, in a larger sense, we can not dedicate—we can not consecrate—we can not hallow—this ground. The brave men, living and dead, who struggled here, have consecrated it, far above our poor power to add or detract. The world will little note, nor long remember what we say here, but it can never forget what they did here. It is for us

Roy P. Basler, ed., *The Collected Works of Abraham Lincoln,* 9 vols. (New Brunswick, N.J.: Rutgers University Press, 1953), 7:22–23. Courtesy of the Abraham Lincoln Association.

the living, rather, to be dedicated here to the unfinished work which they who fought here have thus far so nobly advanced. It is rather for us to be here dedicated to the great task remaining before us—that from these honored dead we take increased devotion to that cause for which they gave the last full measure of devotion—that we here highly resolve that these dead shall not have died in vain—that this nation, under God, shall have a new birth of freedom—and that government of the people, by the people, for the people, shall not perish from the earth.

2

WOODROW WILSON

An Address at the Gettysburg Battlefield

July 4, 1913

The commemoration of the Battle of Gettysburg was the high point of the semicentennial anniversary of the Civil War, featuring a reunion of more than 53,000 Union and Confederate veterans. Wilson (1856–1924), the first southerner to be elected president since the war, was prevailed upon to deliver a brief address on the occasion. He brought to this assignment not only the experience of growing up in the shadow of the war but also the scholarly expertise he had developed in writing a study of the sectional conflict, *Division and Reunion, 1829–1889* (1895). Compare his speech to the address that Lincoln delivered at Gettysburg fifty years earlier. How do the two presidents describe the importance of remembering the events at Gettysburg?

Friends and Fellow Citizens: I need not tell you what the battle of Gettysburg meant. These gallant men in blue and gray sit all about us here. Many of them met here upon this ground in grim and deadly struggle. Upon these famous fields and hillsides their comrades died about them. In their presence it were an impertinence to discourse upon how the battle went, how it ended, what it signified! But fifty years have gone by since then, and I crave the privilege of speaking to you for a few minutes of what those fifty years have meant.

Arthur S. Link, ed., *The Papers of Woodrow Wilson,* 69 vols. (Princeton, N.J.: Princeton University Press, 1966–1994), 28:23–26.

What *have* they meant? They have meant peace and union and vigour, and the maturity and might of a great nation. How wholesome and healing the peace has been! We have found one another again as brothers and comrades in arms, enemies no longer, generous friends rather, our battles long past, the quarrel forgotten—except that we shall not forget the splendid valour, the manly devotion of the men then arrayed against one another, now grasping hands and smiling into each other's eyes. How complete the union has become and how dear to all of us, how unquestioned, how benign and majestic, as state after state has been added to this our great family of free men! How handsome the vigour, the maturity, the might of the great nation we love with undivided hearts; how full of large and confident promise that a life will be wrought out that will crown its strength with gracious justice and with a happy welfare that will touch all alike with deep contentment! We are debtors to those fifty crowded years; they have made us heirs to a mighty heritage. . . .

Look around you upon the field of Gettysburg! Picture the array, the fierce heats and agony of battle, column hurled against column, battery bellowing to battery! Valour? Yes! Greater no man shall see in war; and self-sacrifice, and loss to the uttermost; the high recklessness of exalted devotion which does not count the cost. We are made by these tragic, epic things to know what it costs to make a nation—the blood and sacrifice of multitudes of unknown men lifted to a great stature in the view of all generations by knowing no limit to their manly willingness to serve. In armies thus marshaled from the ranks of free men you will see, as it were, a nation embattled, the leaders and the led, and may know, if you will, how little except in form its action differs in days of peace from its action in days of war.

May we break camp now and be at ease? Are the forces that fight for the nation dispersed, disbanded, gone to their homes forgetful of the common cause? Are our forces disorganized, without constituted leaders and the might of men consciously united because we contend, not with armies, but with principalities and powers and wickedness in high places? Are we content to lie still? . . . War fitted us for action, and action never ceases.

I have been chosen the leader of the nation. I cannot justify the choice by any qualities of my own, but so it has come about, and here I stand. Whom do I command? The ghostly hosts who fought upon these battle fields long ago and are gone? These gallant gentlemen stricken in years whose fighting days are over, their glory won? What are the orders for them, and who rallies them? I have in my mind another host, whom these set free of civil strife in order that they might work out in days of peace and settled order the life of a great nation. That host is the people themselves, the great and the small, without class or difference of kind or race or origin; and undivided in interest, if we have but the vision to guide and direct them and order their lives aright in what we do. Our constitutions are their articles of enlistment. The orders of the day are the laws upon our statute books. What we strive for is their freedom, their right to lift themselves from day to day and behold the things they have hoped for, and so make way for still better days for those whom they love who are to come after them. . . .

CIVIC MONUMENTS

The making of civic monuments was a much more decentralized process than the establishment of battlefield parks. The federal government had little role in civic monument construction outside of Washington, D.C., and the national cemeteries. State governments rarely guided construction of monuments outside of the capital cities, although some states encouraged municipalities to build monuments. Most monuments resulted from initiatives of private individuals and groups. Large cities commissioning expensive monuments often provided government appropriations for them, and some other towns did so as well. In the majority of cases, however, sponsors relied on private donations and fund-raising events for the projects.

The significance of a monument depended in part on the identity of its sponsors. The power to install and dedicate a monument implied authority to shape the public realm and define the conduct that deserved admiration. The soldiers monument unveiled in Oak Bluffs, Massachusetts, in 1891 is a striking example of the extent to which a tribute could reflect back on its sponsor. Proposed as a gesture of sectional reconciliation by former Confederate lieutenant Charles Strahan, the monument to Union soldiers was given an ancillary inscription in 1925 that saluted Confederate soldiers in belated fulfillment of Strahan's wishes. Eventually, residents of Oak Bluff came to understand the monument to be a statue of a Confederate soldier, and it was even painted gray for this reason in the 1970s.

The most striking pattern among promoters of civic monuments was the leadership role assumed by women, expanding well beyond the antebellum record of women's sponsorship of similar projects. Women's groups were active in both the North and the South, but they were more central to commemoration of the Confederacy. Most evident was the regional difference in sponsorship of prominent urban monuments. Northern women did not undertake the conspicuous projects that white southern women conducted in such cities as Augusta, Georgia (1878); Dallas, Texas (1897); and St. Louis, Missouri (1914). The United Daughters of the Confederacy sponsored the high-profile Confederate monument at Arlington National Cemetery (1914) and several monuments to soldiers in battlefield parks, most notably the tribute to Confederate soldiers at Shiloh (1917). The contrast may have reflected not only greater overall commemorative activity among white southern women but also a difference in priorities. For the Women's Relief Corps, sponsorship of monuments occupied a subordinate position on an agenda that also included observance of Memorial Day and campaigns to promote recitation of the Pledge of Allegiance, secure adoption of a national anthem, and fly the American flag over every schoolhouse. In the South, on the other hand, one president-general observed that "memorials are the chief business of the United Daughters of the Confederacy."[2]

3

Soldiers Monuments

1863–1919

The table on page 24 illustrates the distribution of new monument construction across place and time. The data set includes outdoor monuments to rank-and-file Civil War soldiers for which the year of unveiling is known, but it excludes tablets on buildings and monuments in battlefield parks and national cemeteries. It does not include tributes to individuals except when those works explicitly honor a group.[3] The statistics for these sample states roughly parallel the available

Table compiled from information in Benjamin J. Hillman, *Monuments to Memories: Virginia's Civil War Heritage in Bronze and Stone* (Richmond: Virginia Civil War Commission, 1965); George S. May, comp., *Michigan Civil War Monuments* (Lansing: Michigan Civil War Centennial Observance Commission, 1965); David F. Ransom, "Connecticut's Monumental Epoch: A Survey of Civil War Memorials," *Connecticut Historical Society Bulletin* 58 (nos. 1–4, 1993): 6–280; Ralph W. Widener Jr., *Confederate Monuments: Enduring Symbols of the South and the War between the States* (Washington, D.C.: Andromeda Associates, 1982); and Inventory of American Sculpture <http://www.siris.si.edu>, accessed June–August 2001.

regionwide information. How would you account for the different patterns in the Northeast and Midwest, especially in the first years after the war? What might explain the sharp increase in monument construction in the South after 1900?

Known Dates of Unveiling of Soldiers Monuments

DATE	NORTHEAST (CONNECTICUT)	MIDWEST (MICHIGAN)	SOUTH (VIRGINIA)
1863–1879	32	7	10
1880–1899	34	32	34
1900–1919	34	42	83

MONUMENT DESIGNS

The products of independent decisions in thousands of different communities, Civil War monuments inevitably take a wide range of forms, but more striking than that variety is the dominance of one type of composition: the statue of a uniformed standing soldier holding the barrel of a rifle that rests upright on the ground in front of him. Although the poses within these general lines do not conform precisely to a stance prescribed in Civil War manuals of arms, contemporaries often read them as depictions of soldiers at "place rest" or "parade rest." Hundreds of these statues stand on town greens, before courthouses, and in cemeteries throughout the North and South. The emergence of this icon suggests the extent to which Americans with the power to shape commemorative plans reached agreement about how to look back at the Civil War. But the level of consensus is easy to exaggerate. Disagreements often took place over forms of remembrance during the half-century after the war, and popular ideas about the design of monuments went through significant changes. These debates became one of the important ways in which Americans addressed the legacy of the war.

During the 1860s and early 1870s a well-publicized set of soldier statues established a new commemorative style that replaced the obelisk (a tapered pillar) as the dominant type of Civil War monument in the North by the 1880s and in the South by the next decade. Expatriate sculptor Randolph Rogers introduced the soldier statue at Spring Grove cemetery in Cincinnati, depicting a sentinel holding his rifle in a ready position with bayonet fixed (Figure 1-1). Rogers would

Figure 1-1. Randolph Rogers, *Drawing of Proposed Soldiers Monument for Spring Grove Cemetery,* **Cincinnati, ca. 1863.** Why did Americans only begin with the Civil War to commission statues of common soldiers?

Photo courtesy of Bentley Historical Library, University of Michigan.

repeat this design elsewhere, but it would attract few imitators for the next quarter-century.

The Seventh Regiment Memorial in Central Park (Figure 1-2) was an early example of the pose that became standard. Recalling the swift response of the unit to Lincoln's call for troops in April 1861, park architects Frederick Law Olmsted and Calvert Vaux advised sculptor J. Q. A. Ward that "the typical idea represented by the Regiment seems to have been '*Vigilance.*' When the war commenced it was found to be on Guard, prepared for immediate action and ready to take its place as a watchful *Sentinel* in front of the Picketline." Consistent with the familiar image of the isolated picket in wartime songs and poems, Olmsted and Vaux sent sketches designed "to make the central figure of the sentinel look rather lonely and unsupported."[4] Ward's resulting statue of the vigilant citizen-soldier, completed in 1869 and dedicated in 1874, differed sharply from the equally emblematic Revolutionary War counterpart presented in Daniel Chester French's *Minuteman* of 1875 (Figure 1-3). The contrast points to elements that Americans found distinctive in their recent experience.

The physical characteristics no less than the pose of rapidly proliferating soldier statues expressed ideas about the citizen-soldier. Only one known generic single-figure soldier statue, commemorating African American soldiers buried in a cemetery in Norfolk, Virginia, in 1920, clearly appears to represent an African American.[5] Perceived depictions of other ethnic minorities also drew complaints. *Harper's New Monthly* magazine "could but regret" that Rogers chose "a brave Celt" as the model for his Cincinnati sentinel.[6] The monument in Elbert County, Georgia—nicknamed "Dutchy" because local citizens considered it "too German"—was toppled in 1900 and buried facedown to signify military dishonor; a replacement figure was dedicated in 1905.

By the end of the 1880s, almost two hundred single-figure soldier statues had been placed around the country. Moreover, the image had become central to the monument form most often favored by communities aspiring to something grander than a single-figure statue. As early as 1869, Greenwood cemetery in Brooklyn installed an obelisk surrounded by four soldiers. Art critic James Jackson Jarves warned that "soon there will be seen in high place and in low, huge effigies, in bronze and stone, of volunteers on guard at corners of columns, obelisks, and shafts of every conceivable degree of disproportion, misapplication, and inappropriate ornamentation, dedicated to the heroes of our last contest."[7] During the next few years, Providence, Rhode Island (1871), Detroit, Michigan (1872), Worcester (1874) and Boston, Massachusetts (1877), launched the long series of civic monuments that Jarves feared (Figure 1-4). These compositions had several elements, but as Jarves indicated, the figures at the base—often representative of the infantry, the cavalry, the artillery, and the navy—were to many viewers the dominant features.

The convergence of commemorative designs did not result from a lack of alternatives. Debates between the advocates of monuments and proponents of utilitarian memorials posed the most basic choices. A 1910 survey found that twenty-two Massachusetts communities had dedicated libraries, town halls, or other public buildings to Civil War soldiers.[8] Such initiatives often drew vigorous criticism, particularly from veterans. When Harvard University decided to build a grand memorial hall that combined a commemorative vestibule and a dining hall, lawyer John Codman Ropes protested: "Is it a Memorial Hall after all? It is a Dining Hall, called a Memorial Hall. But does calling it a Memorial Hall make it a Memorial Hall? . . . The solemnity which always surrounds death is an essential element in producing the moral impression, which our Memorial is designed to make. Let us not weaken it."[9] Ropes lost at Harvard, but he voiced the prevailing sentiment in postwar America. Although commemorative fountains enjoyed some popularity as a compromise solution, the dedication of memorial buildings was much less common after the Civil War than it would become in public remembrance of World War I soldiers.

Veterans often proposed another alternative to the public monument: a facility in which they might display their relics of the war and conduct meetings. These initiatives had mixed success. Chicago veterans campaigned for years for such a hall in the heart of the city before they managed to lay the cornerstone in 1893. Some other noteworthy reliquaries sprang up around the same time, most notably at the former Confederate White House in Richmond, Virginia (1896). On the whole, however, support for remembrance of the Civil War through museums was weaker than the momentum behind monuments.

Within the genre of figurative monuments, allegorical statues enjoyed strong backing from artists influenced by the Ecole des Beaux-Arts and appeared regularly on monuments in large cities, but

Figure 1-2.   J. Q. A. Ward, *Seventh Infantry Regiment Memorial,*
Central Park, New York City, 1868–1874.
Daniel McPartlin/New York City Parks Photo Archive.

28

Figure 1-3.   Daniel Chester French, *Minute Man,* **Concord, Massachusetts, 1871–1875.**   In what ways was the image of the Civil War soldier different from the image of earlier American soldiers?

Library of Congress.

Figure 1-4. Randolph Rogers, *Michigan Soldiers and Sailors Monument*, **Detroit, 1867–1881.** How was this monument designed to shape the city landscape?

Library of Congress.

allegorical figures often became focal points of public criticism if not accompanied by a soldier statue. As early as 1878, the Ladies Memorial Association of Savannah, Georgia, decided to substitute a soldier statue for the figures of "Silence" and "Judgment" on the Confederate monument the women had dedicated three years earlier; one newspaper noted that the original design "was too symbolic to meet popular approval."[10] Veterans in Jersey City sued (unsuccessfully) to stop the city from erecting Philip Martiny's Soldiers and Sailors Monument (1899) on the grounds that the seated Athena-like figure in helmet and armor could not properly commemorate soldiers.

Statues of specific individuals offered even less competition to the generic soldier as a strategy for remembering collective effort and sacrifice. Relatively few communities followed the example of Lebanon, Tennessee (1912), in which the Confederate monument was a portrait of local politician and fallen officer Robert Hatton. Many inscriptions featured the names or words of national leaders, and a considerable number incorporated portrait reliefs as subordinate elements, but the soldiers monuments taking the form of statues of Stonewall Jackson in Baltimore, Maryland (1870), and Lincoln in Rochester, New York (1892), were unusual. Similarly, generic images of officers were not common. The ordinary private commanded the soldiers monument.

The most widely successful rival to the statue of a soldier at rest eventually proved to be the alternative that Randolph Rogers had introduced during the war: the statue of a more active soldier. In the mid-1880s complaints began to mount that the typical monument did not illustrate "the patriotism, self-sacrifice, bravery and devotion which our soldiers have always displayed" and therefore would not inspire viewers to follow the soldiers' example. A committee in Covington, Kentucky, stipulated in 1894 that it would not accept a figure of a soldier "at parade rest, or one that looks as if he were ashamed that he was a soldier."[11] This dissatisfaction fostered new representations. Only four known single-figure monuments depicted a soldier with the stock of his rifle off the ground before 1890, but at least seventy-seven across the North and South did so between 1890 and 1920. The soldier on the march became a common motif. Theo Alice Ruggles Kitson's *Volunteer of 1861* (Figure 1-5), unveiled at Newburyport, Massachusetts, in 1902, was adopted by eight other communities in

Figure 1-5. T. A. R. Kitson, *Massachusetts Monument, Vicksburg National Military Park (The Volunteer of 1861),* **1901–1902.** Why did statues of active soldiers become more common in the 1890s and following decades?

Library of Congress.

New England, New York, and California.[12] The statue of a flag bearer designed by Launt Thompson for Pittsfield, Massachusetts (1872), was followed by another dozen in the 1880s and almost one hundred more by 1920.

As active figures became more common in single-figure statues, larger communities commissioned monuments featuring groups of active soldiers. In 1888 the mayor of Brooklyn vetoed an appropriation for a standard column surrounded by soldier statues, arguing that the design was "essentially funereal" and failed to "recall to the mind the patriotic pride, the consciousness of sufficient strength which animated and sustained the Nation in that supreme hour."[13] Instead Brooklyn dedicated a triumphal arch (1892) ornamented with dynamic relief ensembles of soldiers and sailors departing for the front, patterned on François Rude's famous *Departure of the Volunteers in 1792* (see Figure 4-4 on page 121) on the Arc de Triomphe in Paris. In addition to such departure scenes, large ensembles of soldiers in combat began to appear on monuments in Cleveland, Ohio (1894); Milwaukee, Wisconsin (1898); and Indianapolis, Indiana (1902). Several of the new compositions, such as Lorado Taft's *Defense of the Flag* for Jackson County, Michigan (Figure 1-6), depicted fallen soldiers, an image that was very rare on monuments dedicated before 1890.

Kitson's *Volunteer of 1861,* which Massachusetts used as its state memorial at Vicksburg, and Taft's *Defense of the Flag,* which the sculptor adapted from a previous version installed at the Chickamauga and Chattanooga National Military Park, indicated the growing similarity of civic and battlefield monuments. Figurative monuments in battlefield parks overwhelmingly tended toward active poses, for these works primarily illustrated events that had taken place on that battlefield. Civic monuments served a wider range of purposes, but sponsors increasingly concluded that these purposes also called for active poses.

Monuments to soldiers of the Spanish-American War and World War I would draw heavily on the models of marching, flag-bearing, fighting, and dying soldiers who emerged in Civil War monuments during the 1890s. This visual tradition would help to inform the rapid public recognition of photographer Joe Rosenthal's picture of Marines raising a flag on Iwo Jima in February 1945 as an image appropriate for translation into the Marine Corps Memorial dedicated outside Washington, D.C., in November 1954.

Figure 1-6. Lorado Taft, *Jackson County Soldiers and Sailors Monument (The Defense of the Flag)*, **Jackson, Michigan, 1894–1904.** How does this ensemble illustrate changing values in Civil War commemoration?

Photo courtesy of Ella Sharp Museum.

If thus superseded in American iconography of the citizen-soldier, the image of the soldier at rest nevertheless remained the central icon of Civil War commemoration. Even during the period from 1890 to 1920, the soldier at rest accounted for over 80 percent of known single-figure monuments. Economic considerations alone cannot account for this popularity. Monuments suppliers offered a variety of designs at competitive prices, and trade journals strongly criticized the supposed passivity of the image of the soldier at rest. But the soldier at rest was evidently an image that appealed to the sponsors of monuments. Two leading scholars have advanced strikingly different interpretations of this phenomenon. Gaines Foster has proposed that "the passionless soldier" embodied the "disciplined, loyal supporter of society" desired by business and political elites who sponsored monuments in an era of industrialization and social tension. Kirk Savage has argued that the pose "offered a compromise between regimentation and independence" that, together with the racialized features of the common soldier and his representation as an individual rather than as part of a group, helped to relieve a disquieting social recognition that military discipline resembled slavery.[14] The interpretations suggest the extent to which the soldier statue left open a range of debate over its meaning at the same time that it both promoted and discouraged other possible visions of the American self in the wake of the Civil War.

MONUMENT INSCRIPTIONS

Monument sponsors often devoted even more attention to their inscription than to their design, and their efforts produced a wider range of results. But amid the variety a loose set of conventions and repeated formulations emerged, some of which Union and Confederate monuments shared and some of which were characteristic of one side.

The most basic purposes of the inscription were to identify its originators and those to whom it was dedicated. Inscriptions on Civil War monuments almost always identified the sponsors, unlike the monuments dedicated by French communities in remembrance of World War I soldiers, which rarely referred to the processes that produced the tribute. An explicit statement of local sponsorship was crucial to the idea of most town and county monuments. Similarly, the central role of women in many monument campaigns was too important, both to those women and to men, not to be recorded on the memorials. Potentially more controversial were inscriptions identifying individuals who had donated monuments. When circus promoter Dan Rice had his name chiseled into a monument that he presented to Erie County, Pennsylvania, in a highly publicized spectacle in November 1865, a local newspaper asked whether the obelisk was "a memorial to the dead, or an advertisement of the living."[15] But in both the North and the South, monuments given by individuals continued to bear the names of patrons who sought to imprint their authority in the public imagination.

Most soldiers monuments not placed in battlefield parks honored soldiers and sailors from the town, county, or state in which the monument was erected. During and immediately after the war, monuments were usually dedicated to the dead, but in the North new monuments dedicated to all soldiers who had served began during the 1880s to outnumber those dedicated to men who had died. The same change did not take place in the South until the first decade of the twentieth century.[16]

Many civic monuments listed the names of soldiers from the community. Even on monuments dedicated to all who had fought, the list usually identified only the dead, although in some cases it included the names of everyone who had entered military service. Compilation of such a list could be a daunting and delicate exercise. The committee that sponsored the Cuyahoga County Soldiers and Sailors Monument in Cleveland, Ohio (1894), circulated 10,000 copies of a list of local veterans before carving the names of 9,000 soldiers from the county on a wall of the monument.[17] Some monuments listed soldiers by rank, but alphabetical order was much more common. Scattered throughout both sections are monuments dedicated to the "unknown dead," precursors to the shrines to unknown soldiers established in Europe and the United States after World War I.

Beyond the common goals of identifying sponsors and those whom monuments honored, Union and Confederate inscriptions also expressed some of the same sentiments. Monuments for both sides quoted the Horatian adage "Dulce et decorum est pro patria more" ("It is sweet and proper to die for one's country"). Much more common were excerpts from Theodore O'Hara's poem "The Bivouac of the Dead" (ca. 1850), a tribute to fallen soldiers of the Mexican-

American War. The widely quoted first verse of the poem suggests the framework through which many Americans sought to comprehend death in the Civil War:

> The muffled drum's sad roll has beat
> The soldier's last tattoo;
> No more on life's parade shall meet
> That brave and fallen few.
> On Fame's eternal camping-ground
> Their silent tents are spread,
> And Glory guards, with solemn round,
> The bivouac of the dead.

Each side also developed a distinctive repertory of rhetorical strategies for inscriptions. Of the texts quoted exclusively on Union monuments, the Gettysburg Address appeared most often. Other favorites included Lincoln's Second Inaugural Address, Webster's promise of "liberty and union," Ulysses S. Grant's slogan "Let us have peace," and President James A. Garfield's declaration that "the war for the Union was right, everlastingly right, and the war against the Union was wrong, forever wrong." The Grand Army of the Republic and its affiliates inscribed their shared motto "Fraternity, Charity, Loyalty" on monuments throughout the North. Also common was the slogan "One Country, One Flag, One Destiny," an adaptation of Webster's call for "one country, one constitution, one destiny" that reflected the new heart of American patriotic symbolism.

Whether or not they quoted the Gettysburg Address, many Union inscriptions joined Lincoln in juxtaposing the death faced by soldiers and the permanence achieved by the United States. Milford, Connecticut, was typical in dedicating its 1888 monument "TO THE MEMORY OF THE MEN / WHO RISKED THEIR LIVES THAT / THE NATION MIGHT LIVE." Far fewer monuments followed Lincoln in connecting this national life to a new birth; instead "preservation" was a key word in inscriptions. Apart from those that included the end of the Gettysburg Address, less than 5 percent of known Union inscriptions refer explicitly to the abolition of slavery as an achievement celebrated by the monument. Saugus, Massachusetts (1875), and Manchester (1878) and Antrim, New Hampshire (1892), are rare examples of monuments that identity "equal rights" as an objective of the war.

On the whole, Confederate inscriptions were more extensive than their Union counterparts and were written in a higher emotional pitch. Some monuments dedicated by the Women's Relief Corps expressed "loving remembrance" of Union soldiers, but declarations of love and "tender reverence" for soldiers were routine on Confederate monuments, beginning with the many inscriptions that incorporated the motto of the United Daughters of the Confederacy: "Love Makes Memory Eternal." Unable to point to final victory as proof of military achievement, Confederate tributes emphasized much more strenuously that the honored soldiers had, in the words of the St. Louis monument (1914), "PERFORMED DEEDS / OF PROWESS SUCH AS / THRILLED THE HEART OF / MANKIND WITH ADMIRATION / . . . . / AND DISPLAYED A COURAGE / SO SUPERB / THAT IT GAVE A NEW AND / BRIGHTER LUSTER TO THE / ANNALS OF VALOR."

While most Union inscriptions simply stated the supposed motives of soldiers with the expectation that the reader would approve of them, Confederate inscriptions often praised the purity of soldiers' motives without explaining what those motives were. Among monuments that elaborated on the theme of Confederate purity, Randolph Harrison McKim's inscription on the monument in Arlington National Cemetery (1914) illustrated a cautious strategy: "NOT FOR FAME OR REWARD / NOT FOR PLACE OR FOR RANK / NOT LURED BY AMBITION / OR GOADED BY NECESSITY / BUT IN SIMPLE / OBEDIENCE TO DUTY / AS THEY UNDERSTOOD IT / THESE MEN SUFFERED ALL / SACRIFICED ALL / DARED ALL AND DIED." A few Confederate inscriptions borrowed or paralleled McKim's words, but the Jacksonville, Alabama (1909), monument expressed a widely shared sentiment with a quotation from Jefferson Davis: "LET NONE OF THE SURVIVORS OF / THESE MEN OFFER IN THEIR / BEHALF THE PENITENTIAL PLEA / 'THEY BELIEVED THEY WERE / RIGHT.' "

More specific statements of the Confederate cause overwhelmingly stressed local autonomy. "Patriotism" was a key word on southern monuments, and inscriptions often characterized the soldiers as defending their homes against invasion. The monument in St. Francisville, Louisiana (1903), mourned that "THE DUST OF OUR HEROES HATH / HALLOWED THE SOD / WHERE THEY STRUGGLED FOR RIGHT / AND FOR HOME AND FOR GOD." Dozens of inscriptions raised constitutional arguments, usually couched in terms of "states' rights" or "local self-government" but sometimes more broadly through allusions to "constitutional liberty" or "constitutional government." Such inscriptions began to appear as early as the dedication of monuments in Athens (1872) and Augusta (1878), Georgia, but constitutional argument became more common in inscriptions during the later stage of southern monument-building.

Few southern monuments directly addressed the issues of race and slavery that had been central to the coming of the war and to Confederate ideology. Reference to "faithful slaves" on soldiers monuments in Columbia, North Carolina (1902), and Chesterfield, South Carolina (1928), supplemented the monuments to "faithful slaves" at Fort Mill, South Carolina (1896), and Natchitoches, Louisiana (1927). Several Confederate inscriptions celebrated a theme implicit in many of the monuments: that after the war southern whites had prevailed over attempts to reconstruct the social order. Milledgeville, Georgia (1912), noted that Confederate soldiers' "UNCONQUERABLE / PATRIOTISM AND SELF- / SACRIFICE RENDERED / ABORTIVE THE EFFORT / OF HIS ENEMIES / AFTER HIS FLAG HAD / FOLDED FOREVER TO / DESTROY HIS PROUD / INHERITANCE."[18] The monument in Obion County, Tennessee (1909), thanked the Confederate soldier "WHO HAS PRESERVED ANGLO-SAXON CIVILIZATION / IN THE SOUTH."

Confederate monuments incorporated a larger repertory of distinctive texts than Union monuments. Commonplace references to "our Confederate dead" or "our Confederate heroes" had no clear parallel in the North. Confederate inscriptions also included far more quotations from poetry. For example, Corinth, Mississippi (1896), and Montgomery (1898) and Athens, Alabama (1909), featured Francis Orray Ticknor's tribute in "The Virginians of the Valley" to "the knightliest knights of the knightly race / Who, since the days of old, / Have kept the lamp of chivalry / Alight in hearts of gold." Catholic priest Abram J. Ryan (1838–1886) was the poet-laureate of the Confederate monument. Numerous inscriptions quoted his works "The Sword of Robert E. Lee" (Document 11), "The Conquered Banner," "C.S.A.," and "Sentinel Songs." The lines by Ryan most frequently quoted on Confederate monuments were the first and fourth verses of "The March of the Deathless Dead":

> Gather the sacred dust
> Of the warriors tried and true.
> Who bore the flag of a Nation's trust
> And fell in a cause, though lost, still just,
> And died for me and you.
>
> . . . .

> We care not whence they came,
>   Dear in their lifeless clay!
> Whether unknown, or known to fame,
> Their cause and country still the same;
>   They died—and wore the Gray.

Such inscriptions helped to canonize texts that constituted a key element of the culture of the Lost Cause.

4

WILLIAM HENRY TRESCOT

Inscription on South Carolina Soldiers Monument

1879

Historian and diplomat William Henry Trescot (1822–1898) was one of the leading intellectuals of the South Carolina planter elite. He was a member of the South Carolina legislature and the state executive council during the war and was an important voice of lowcountry planter interests during Reconstruction. His inscription for the monument to the Confederate dead of South Carolina is unique among Civil War monument inscriptions in that it added a major new text to the canon of commemorative literature. At least ten monuments around the South borrowed from Trescot's inscription, and it appeared in southern literary anthologies. What meaning does it find in the deaths the monument remembers?

(Front)
THIS MONUMENT
PERPETUATES THE MEMORY,
OF THOSE WHO
TRUE TO THE INSTINCTS OF THEIR BIRTH,
FAITHFUL TO THE TEACHINGS OF THEIR FATHERS,
CONSTANT IN THEIR LOVE FOR THE STATE,
DIED IN THE PERFORMANCE OF THEIR DUTY;
WHO
HAVE GLORIFIED A FALLEN CAUSE
BY THE SIMPLE MANHOOD OF THEIR LIVES,
THE PATIENT ENDURANCE OF SUFFERING,

AND THE HEROISM OF DEATH,
AND WHO,
IN THE DARK HOURS OF IMPRISONMENT,
IN THE HOPELESSNESS OF THE HOSPITAL,
IN THE SHORT, SHARP AGONY OF THE FIELD,
FOUND SUPPORT AND CONSOLATION
IN THE BELIEF
THAT AT HOME THEY WOULD NOT BE FORGOTTEN.

(Rear)
LET THE STRANGER,
WHO MAY IN FUTURE TIMES
READ THIS INSCRIPTION,
RECOGNIZE THAT THESE WERE MEN
WHOM POWER COULD NOT CORRUPT,
WHOM DEATH COULD NOT TERRIFY,
WHOM DEFEAT COULD NOT DISHONOR,
AND LET THEIR VIRTUES PLEAD
FOR JUST JUDGMENT
OF THE CAUSE IN WHICH THEY PERISHED.
LET THE SOUTH CAROLINIAN
OF ANOTHER GENERATION
REMEMBER
THAT THE STATE TAUGHT THEM
HOW TO LIVE AND HOW TO DIE,
AND THAT FROM HER BROKEN FORTUNES
SHE HAS PRESERVED FOR HER CHILDREN
THE PRICELESS TREASURE OF THEIR MEMORIES,
TEACHING ALL WHO MAY CLAIM
THE SAME BIRTHRIGHT
THAT TRUTH, COURAGE, AND PATRIOTISM
ENDURE FOREVER.

RITUALS OF REMEMBRANCE

Prescribed practices of commemoration consecrated the places of Civil War memory. The dedication of a monument was one of the three basic ceremonies of remembrance during the half-century after the war, along with Memorial Day and the veterans reunion. The three events might coincide, as at the 1907 dedication of the J. E. B. Stuart Monument in Richmond on the date of a local observance of Confederate Memorial Day during an annual meeting of the United Confederate

Veterans. But the rituals differed significantly in their structures and key participants, providing instruments for negotiating several different tensions in remembrance of the war.

The development of Memorial Day was the most complicated of these partially overlapping histories. The core of the ritual as it emerged in several locations in the North and South in the immediate aftermath of the war was the decoration of soldiers' graves with spring flowers, an adaptation of a mourning practice that had become commonplace in the mid nineteenth century. The custom may have originated in European celebrations of All Saints' Day, and observers routinely compared Memorial Day to that Christian holy day and also to Easter. Standard observance of the occasion soon incorporated a church service, either on Memorial Day or on the preceding Sunday, and a procession to the cemetery for prayers, hymns, and the decoration of graves. Women were usually the most prominent participants in the ceremony. In the former Confederacy women also organized the event, which took place on different dates in different communities, the most common of which were May 10, the anniversary of the death of Stonewall Jackson, and June 3, the birthday of Jefferson Davis. Union women shared authority over Memorial Day with veterans to a greater extent, for in 1868 Grand Army of the Republic commander John A. Logan ordered all posts to take charge of annual local observance on May 30. In both versions of Memorial Day, however, the decoration of graves by women placed remembrance of soldiers in a familial and religious context.

Logan's circular of 1868 presaged important shifts in the observance of Memorial Day in both sections. Coordination expanded as the occasion began to be recognized as a legal holiday, first in New York in 1873, by the federal government in 1876, and almost all northern states by 1890. Moreover, orations soon became more central to commemoration, quickly building a prime platform for debate over political issues related to the war. Invited to deliver a Memorial Day address in Brooklyn, New York, in 1877, former Confederate general Roger A. Pryor claimed that Reconstruction had been characterized by "usurpations of force on the popular will and the independence of the States" and called for equal recognition of the valor of Confederate soldiers. The next year, Frederick Douglass responded in a Memorial Day address in Madison Square Garden that "there was a right side and a wrong side in the late war, which no sentiment ought to cause us to forget" and looked ahead to when the Americans would again "stand as a wall of fire around the Republic, and in the end see Liberty, Equality, and Justice triumphant." By 1880, the *New York Tribune* complained that Memorial Day had fallen into "the slough of politics."[19]

Douglass's acknowledgment that "pageantry is better than oratory" on Memorial Day spoke to another trend in the ritual: the rise of the parade as an element of a more celebratory observance in the mid 1870s in both the North and the South. These spectacles tended to turn the focus of the ritual away from civilians, and particularly women, but no simple transformation took place. Early parades featured civic and church groups as well as veterans and active military units. Decoration of graves remained the hallmark of the day, and the growth of the Women's Relief Corps in the early 1880s expanded women's presence in Union observances. Debates over the name of the holiday reflected the contest. Veterans from both sides insisted on the original name Memorial Day, but the alternative Decoration Day remained in common use through the late nineteenth century, especially for the northern commemoration.

While Memorial Day provided a structure for addressing the soldier's ties to his society, the citizenship of women and African Americans, and the relationship between religion and the state, perhaps the most enduring theme in the history of the holiday became its position in the national calendar of leisure and consumption. By the 1890s northern and southern veterans frequently lamented that too many Americans devoted the day to recreation rather than remembrance. Athletic events held on Memorial Day were one locus of controversy, often denounced by veterans as too frivolous for the solemn occasion. No less problematic were special holiday promotions of merchandise for sale. Memorial Day orators described themselves as interrupting the acquisitive and indulgent practices of everyday life to reflect on the nonmaterialistic virtues that they identified with the Civil War soldier. This theme inevitably led to collisions with the economic impulses that helped to drive Civil War commemoration, as when Joseph R. Lamar declared in a Memorial Day address in Athens, Georgia, in 1902 that "Confederate soldiers cry out from the grave for Southerners to . . . diversify our products and to keep step to the great industrial march of the age."[20]

Veterans' reunions involved fewer controversies over control of the ritual and highlighted a different set of issues. The major gatherings of the Grand Army of the Republic and United Confederate Veterans were organized by veterans, although the events also drew many non-veterans. About 12,000 ex-soldiers traveled to Dallas for the 1902 meeting of the UCV, at which the total number of visitors was estimated at 140,000. The reunions were, as one contemporary observed, "the annual festival of the South."[21] In both North and South, the events fit comfortably into the commercial economy, as cities vied to host the large crowds. The festivity of these occasions and the convergence of memory and business brought onto a regional or statewide stage the entrepreneurial networking that figured prominently in the everyday relations of local UCV and GAR units.

Like many other aspects of the veterans groups, the reunions encapsulated tensions between camaraderie and rank in memory of the Civil War, or between democracy and hierarchy in postwar society. The egalitarianism of the veterans groups reached its peak in the carnival atmosphere of the reunion. The nostalgic reminiscences, singing of war songs, and the admiration of war relics that strengthened fellowship in local gatherings of veterans were heightened by the scale of the annual meeting and the shared pleasure of sitting at the center of public attention. The veterans parade, the centerpiece of reunions, often displayed irreverence toward the official discipline of the military march. At the same time, the reunion provided reminders of the realities of hierarchy, not least of which was the veterans' own fascination with the celebrity of the war commanders. The awareness that the reunion marked a departure from everyday life served to reinforce the relations of power that the event temporarily relaxed.

Monument dedications ranged between the solemnity of Memorial Day and the festivity of the veterans reunion, offering a flexible ritual for the negotiation of social tensions. Orchestration of the ceremony could involve many different groups, such as monument sponsors, civic associations, public officials, veterans, and local merchants. Some dedications were funereal in style, and ministers often delivered the early dedicatory addresses. Other monument dedications were highly celebratory, focusing more on a parade than on the oration or the unveiling. Ceremonies could draw enormous crowds and constitute veterans' reunions comparable in scale to an annual meeting of the Grand Army of the Republic or the United Confederate Veterans. Dedication orations were highly publicized speaking engagements, which monument committees usually turned over to veterans and political leaders. Whether mournful or festive, monument dedications were designed to be memorable occasions, and organizers often published the proceedings. Remembrance of the dedication created a complex interplay with remembrance of the events that the monument honored, sometimes deepening and sometimes displacing the initial impulse behind the commemoration.

The dedication was not necessarily the final ritual to focus on a monument, for these structures aimed to shape the symbolic life of a community. For example, Civil War monuments naturally became an element of Memorial Day ceremonies in many towns. The careers of the monuments after unveiling reflected a potential for long-term vitality that was only partly set in stone at the dedication.

5

OLIVER WENDELL HOLMES JR.

The Soldier's Faith

May 30, 1895

A line officer in the 20th Massachusetts Regiment, which participated in much of the hardest fighting of the war, Holmes (1841–1935) was wounded three times. His commitment to what he called "the Christian crusade of the 19th century" and his ideals of military service struggled against his fears and his sense of guilt that he had survived while so many comrades had not. When his three-year commitment expired in July 1864, he began the studies that led to one of the most important careers in the history of American jurisprudence. This Memorial Day address, delivered at Harvard Memorial Hall in 1895, is a sweeping statement of the lessons of the war in retrospect, a perspective that Holmes contrasts with his wartime viewpoint. Theodore

Oliver Wendell Holmes, *Speeches* (Boston: Little, Brown and Company, 1913), 56–66.

Roosevelt's admiration for the speech may have contributed to his decision to appoint Holmes to the United States Supreme Court in 1902. What does Holmes describe as the moral significance of the citizen-soldier? What is the religious perspective of this reflection on faith?

Any day in Washington Street, when the throng is greatest and busiest, you may see a blind man playing a flute. I suppose that some one hears him. Perhaps also my pipe may reach the heart of some passer in the crowd.

I once heard a man say, "Where Vanderbilt sits, there is the head of the table. I teach my son to be rich." He said what many think. For although the generation born about 1840, and now governing the world, has fought two at least of the greatest wars in history, and has witnessed others, war is out of fashion, and the man who commands the attention of his fellows is the man of wealth. Commerce is the great power. The aspirations of the world are those of commerce. Moralists and philosophers, following its lead, declare that war is wicked, foolish, and soon to disappear.

The society for which many philanthropists, labor reformers, and men of fashion unite in longing is one in which they may be comfortable and may shine without much trouble or any danger. The unfortunately growing hatred of the poor for the rich seems to me to rest on the belief that money is the main thing (a belief in which the poor have been encouraged by the rich), more than on any grievance. Most of my hearers would rather that their daughters or their sisters should marry a son of one of the great rich families than a regular army officer, were he as beautiful, brave, and gifted as Sir William Napier.* I have heard the question asked whether our war was worth fighting, after all. There are many, poor and rich, who think that love of country is an old wife's tale, to be replaced by interest in a labor union, or under the name of cosmopolitanism, by a rootless self-seeking search for a place where the most enjoyment may be had at the least cost.

Meantime we have learned the doctrine that evil means pain, and the revolt against pain in all its forms has grown more and more marked. From societies for the prevention of cruelty to animals up to socialism, we express in numberless ways the notion that suffering is a wrong which can be and ought to be prevented, and a whole literature of sympathy has sprung into being which points out in story and in verse how hard it is to be wounded in the battle of life, how terrible, how unjust it is that any one should fail.

Even science has had its part in the tendencies which we observe. It has shaken established religion in the minds of very many. It has pur-

---

*Sir William Napier (1785–1860) was a British military commander and author of the *History of the War in the Peninsula* (6 vols., 1828–1840).

sued analysis until at last this thrilling world of colors and sounds and passions has seemed fatally to resolve itself into one vast network of vibrations endlessly weaving an aimless web, and the rainbow flush of cathedral windows, which once to enraptured eyes appeared the very smile of God, fades slowly out into the pale irony of the void.

And yet from vast orchestras still comes the music of mighty symphonies. Our painters even now are spreading along the walls of our Library glowing symbols of mysteries still real, and the hardly silenced cannon of the East proclaim once more that combat and pain still are the portion of man.* For my own part, I believe that the struggle for life is the order of the world, at which it is vain to repine. I can imagine the burden changed in the way in which it is to be borne, but I cannot imagine that it ever will be lifted from men's backs. I can imagine a future in which science shall have passed from the combative to the dogmatic stage, and shall have gained such catholic acceptance that it shall take control of life, and condemn at once with instant execution what now is left for nature to destroy. But we are far from such a future, and we cannot stop to amuse or to terrify ourselves with dreams. Now, at least, and perhaps as long as man dwells upon the globe, his destiny is battle, and he has to take the chances of war. If it is our business to fight, the book for the army is a war-song, not a hospital-sketch.† It is not well for soldiers to think much about wounds. Sooner or later we shall fall; but meantime it is for us to fix our eyes upon the point to be stormed, and to get there if we can.

Behind every scheme to make the world over, lies the question, What kind of a world do you want? The ideals of the past for men have been drawn from war, as those for women have been drawn from motherhood. For all our prophecies, I doubt if we are ready to give up our inheritance. Who is there who would not like to be thought a gentleman? Yet what has that name been built on but the soldier's choice of honor rather than life? To be a soldier or descended from soldiers, in time of peace to be ready to give one's life rather than to suffer disgrace, that is what the word has meant; and if we try to claim it at less cost than a splendid carelessness for life, we are trying to steal the good will without the responsibilities of the place. We will not dispute about tastes. The man of the future may want something different. But who of us could endure a world, although cut up into five-acre lots and having no man upon it who was not well fed and well housed, without the divine folly of honor, without the senseless passion for knowledge outreaching the flaming bounds of the possible, without ideals the essence of which is that they never can be achieved? I do not know what is true.

---

*Holmes refers to the recent unveiling of the first segments of Edwin Abbey's mural series *The Holy Grail* and John Singer Sargent's *The World's Religions* in the Boston Public Library and to the end of the Sino-Japanese War.
†Holmes alludes to Louisa May Alcott's popular novella *Hospital Sketches* (1863).

I do not know the meaning of the universe. But in the midst of doubt, in the collapse of creeds, there is one thing I do not doubt, that no man who lives in the same world with most of us can doubt, and that is that the faith is true and adorable which leads a soldier to throw away his life in obedience to a blindly accepted duty, in a cause which he little understands, in a plan of campaign of which he has no notion, under tactics of which he does not see the use.

Most men who know battle know the cynic force with which the thoughts of common-sense will assail them in times of stress; but they know that in their greatest moments faith has trampled those thoughts under foot. If you have been in line, suppose on Tremont Street Mall, ordered simply to wait and to do nothing, and have watched the enemy bring their guns to bear upon you down a gentle slope like that from Beacon Street,* have seen the puff of the firing, have felt the burst of the spherical case-shot as it came toward you, have heard and seen the shrieking fragments go tearing through your company, and have known that the next or the next shot carries your fate; if you have advanced in line and have seen ahead of you the spot which you must pass where the rifle bullets are striking; if you have ridden by night at a walk toward the blue line of fire at the dead angle of Spottsylvania, where for twenty-four hours the soldiers were fighting on the two sides of an earthwork, and in the morning the dead and dying lay piled in a row six deep, and as you rode have heard the bullets splashing in the mud and earth about you; if you have been on the picket-line at night in a black and unknown wood, have heard the spat of the bullets upon the trees, and as you moved have felt your foot slip upon a dead man's body; if you have had a blind fierce gallop against the enemy, with your blood up and a pace that left no time for fear,—if, in short, as some, I hope many, who hear me, have known, you have known the vicissitudes of terror and of triumph in war, you know that there is such a thing as the faith I spoke of. You know your own weakness and are modest; but you know that man has in him that unspeakable somewhat which makes him capable of miracle, able to lift himself by the might of his own soul, unaided, able to face annihilation for a blind belief. . . .

War, when you are at it, is horrible and dull. It is only when time has passed that you see that its message was divine. I hope it may be long before we are called again to sit at that master's feet. But some teacher of the kind we all need. In this snug, over-safe corner of the world we need it, that we may realize that our comfortable routine is no eternal necessity of things, but merely a little space of calm in the midst of the tempestuous untamed streaming of the world, and in order that we may be ready for danger. We need it in this time of individualist negations, with its literature of French and American humor, revolting at disci-

---

*Tremont Street and Beacon Street form opposite sides of Boston Common.

pline, loving flesh-pots, and denying that anything is worthy of reverence,—in order that we may remember all that buffoons forget. We need it everywhere and at all times. For high and dangerous action teaches us to believe as right beyond dispute things for which our doubting minds are slow to find words of proof. Out of heroism grows faith in the worth of heroism. The proof comes later, and even may never come. Therefore I rejoice at every dangerous sport which I see pursued. The students at Heidelberg, with their sword-slashed faces, inspire me with sincere respect. I gaze with delight upon our polo-players. If once in a while in our rough riding a neck is broken, I regard it, not as a waste, but as a price well paid for the breeding of a race fit for headship and command.

We do not save our traditions, in this country. The regiments whose battle-flags were not large enough to hold the names of the battles they had fought, vanished with the surrender of Lee, although their memories inherited would have made heroes for a century. It is the more necessary to learn the lesson afresh from perils newly sought, and perhaps it is not vain for us to tell the new generation what we learned in our day, and what we still believe. That the joy of life is living, is to put out all one's powers as far as they will go; that the measure of power is obstacles overcome; to ride boldly at what is in front of you, be it fence or enemy; to pray, not for comfort, but for combat; to keep the soldier's faith against the doubts of civil life, more besetting and harder to overcome than all the misgivings of the battle-field, and to remember that duty is not to be proved in the evil day, but then to be obeyed unquestioning; to love glory more than the temptations of wallowing ease, but to know that one's final judge and only rival is oneself: with all our failures in act and thought, these things we learned from noble enemies in Virginia or Georgia or on the Mississippi, thirty years ago; these things we believe to be true. . . .

CONTEMPORARY COMMEMORATIONS

The forms of remembrance of the Civil War soldier changed significantly in the mid twentieth century. To be sure, some forms of memory remained vital and contested. The network of battlefield parks continued to expand and to face familiar issues, such as the distribution of emphasis between reconstructing scenes of combat and representing the sources of the conflict; legislation adopted by Congress in 2000 directed all battle sites maintained by the National Park Service "to recognize . . . the unique role that the institution of slavery played in causing the Civil War."[22] Another recurrent tension centered on the relationship between preservation of battlefields and surrounding land uses. The proposal of the Walt Disney Corporation in the mid 1990s to place an American history theme park next to the Manassas National Battlefield Park prompted a searching debate over the economic and educational values of battlefield parks, culminating in abandonment of the plans to build Disney's America.

But many forms of memory did not share the continuity seen in battlefield parks. Dedications of new civic monuments fell sharply during the 1920s, although previously installed monuments still helped to shape the commemorative landscape. Civil War veterans' organizations gradually faded away. Memorial Day and some military cemeteries, such as Arlington National Cemetery, came to be associated more broadly with American soldiers than with the Civil War alone.

New forms of remembrance emerged in the second half of the twentieth century. One striking development was the rise of the practice of "reenacting" the experiences of common soldiers. Former Civil War soldiers were their own first reenactors; the presentation of sentimental scenes of camp life was a favorite activity of veterans' groups. The Civil War centennial of 1961–1965 marked the early stages of reenacting as a sophisticated costumed role-playing activity comparable to the presentations long familiar at sites like Colonial Williamsburg and Plimoth Plantation. Discouraged by Civil War centennial organizers as irreverent, reenacting gained considerably in popularity during the American Revolution Bicentennial of 1976–1983 and the one hundred twenty-fifth anniversary of the Civil War. By 1998 an estimated 40,000 Americans engaged in the rapidly growing hobby of Civil War reenacting.[23] Described by participants as tributes to the common soldier and the women allied with him, presentations of encampments and battles offered a parallel to the commemorations provided by public monuments in the late nineteenth and early twentieth centuries. The contrasts between these tributes, both in form and content, offered a revealing measure of shifts in American culture.

It was no coincidence that Confederate reenactors vastly outnumbered Union reenactors, as remembrance of the Confederate common soldier flourished in other forms as well. The Sons of Confederate Veterans, a feeble organization for decades after its founding in 1896, experienced a rejuvenation. One authority reported that the North Carolina SCV had only 500 members in 1986 and more than 3,000 by 1997.[24]

Display of the battle flag under which many Confederates fought has been in recent years the most controversial form of commemoration associated with the citizen-soldier of the Civil War. The "Southern Cross" emblem adopted by the Army of Northern Virginia in the fall of 1861 served during the war as the leading Confederate symbol of soldiers' sacrifices and in 1863 was incorporated into the second national flag of the Confederacy, the "Stainless Banner," which replaced the "Stars and Bars" that had come to be deemed too similar to the Stars and Stripes of the United States.[25] Commonplace at Confederate veterans' reunions and monument dedications, the Southern Cross remained visible afterward on white southern college campuses and in occasional other contexts before reemerging as a high-profile symbol in the "Dixiecrat" presidential campaign of 1948 that protested President Harry Truman's federal civil rights policy. In the next few years the image diffused more widely, as youth culture made the Rebel banner one of the hallmark fads of the early 1950s. With the U.S. Supreme Court decision in *Brown v. Board of Education* (1954), opponents of racial integration—including but not limited to militant white supremacist groups like the Ku Klux Klan—raised the Southern Cross in protest.[26]

Conflicts over display of the Southern Cross have sometimes centered on the rights of individuals, as in cases testing the authority of public school officials to bar students from wearing the emblem, but the most heated controversies have centered on state uses of the symbol. Mississippi incorporated the Southern Cross into its flag in 1895, and Georgia did so in 1956. South Carolina and Alabama began to fly the Southern Cross over their state capitols in the early 1960s, and other states displayed the flag on the statehouse grounds. Protests against these decisions strengthened markedly in the last quarter of the twentieth century, culminating in removal of the Southern Cross from atop the Alabama and South Carolina capitols, a contested redesign of the Georgia flag, and a Mississippi referendum in which a proposal to adopt a new state flag was defeated. In the early twenty-first century, no issue of commemoration more clearly illustrates the continued presence of the Civil War in American culture.

6

NAACP

Resolution on Confederate Battle Flag and Emblem

2001

In 1991 the annual national convention of the National Association for the Advancement of Colored People (NAACP) adopted a resolution committing the organization to seek removal of the Southern Cross from all public properties. This document summarizes the main arguments advanced by the NAACP in protests against public display of the emblem. What different approaches to interpretation of the Southern Cross do the three paragraphs of the preamble illustrate? Do you believe that Mississippi should change its state flag to eliminate the Southern Cross (see Figure 2-5) and that South Carolina should cease flying the banner on the grounds of its state house?

5a. Re-affirming the 2000 Resolution on the Confederate Battle Flag and the Confederate Battle Emblem

WHEREAS, the Confederate States of America came into being by way of secession from the United States of America out of a desire to defend the right of individual states to maintain an economic system based on slave labor; and

WHEREAS, the Confederate Battle Flag and Confederate Battle Emblem have been embraced as the primary symbols for the numerous modern-day groups advocating white supremacy; and

WHEREAS, the Confederate Battle Flag and Confederate Battle Emblem in its present position of display makes a statement of public policy that continues to be an affront to the sensibilities and dignity of a majority of Americans.

THEREFORE, BE IT RESOLVED, that the National Association for the Advancement of Colored People at its 91st Annual Convention reaffirm its condemnation . . . of the Confederate Battle Flag or the Confederate

Resolution Adopted at 91st Annual NAACP Convention Reaffirming 2000 Resolution on the Confederate Battle Flag and Confederate Battle Emblem. The publisher wishes to thank the National Association for the Advancement of Colored People for authorizing the use of this work.

Battle Emblem being flown over, displayed in or on any public site or space, building, or any emblem, flag standard or as part of any public communication. . . .

7

CHARLEY REESE

Purge South of Its Symbols?
You're Barking Up Wrong Flagpole
1997

This editorial illustrates the most common defenses of state display of the Southern Cross, including an emphasis that the flag is a symbol of the Confederate soldier. What tactics does Reese adopt in supporting display of the emblem on public property? To what extent does his argument for Confederate commemoration resemble the ideas advanced by Trescot and other authors of inscriptions on Confederate monuments?

Some Yankees and Southern scalawags won't quit fighting the Civil War—at least the Reconstruction part. They want to purge the South of the Confederate flag, Confederate monuments and other historic symbols.

Well, we Southerners have always been willing to be reconciled, but we won't be reconstructed. We are not going to allow people to obliterate our history and its symbols. We strongly advise our fellow Americans in other parts of the republic to defend their history and their symbols. . . .

I'll tell you why Southerners defend these symbols. The best way to do that is to address the lies told about those symbols.

The Confederate battle flag is not a racist symbol. I understand perfectly that any black person who has had it waved in his or her face by some 20th-century racist, would consider it in that light. But 20th-century yahoos have nothing to do with the 300,000 men who fought and died for that flag in the 19th century.

Orlando Sentinel, February 20, 1997. Reprinted with special permission of King Features Syndicate.

Those men did not fight a race war. They did not even fight, as many think, to preserve slavery. They fought for Southern independence and for the constitutional republic created in 1787, which they believed that Northern states had betrayed.

That's better understood if you get rid of the Hollywood images of the Old South. Watching movies or television, you would think that there was no one in the South except rich plantation owners and slaves. Nothing could be further from the truth. In 1860, there were 7 million whites in the South, and 6.6 million of them did not own a single slave. There were 250,000 free blacks living in the 15 slave states. Some of them owned slaves. Five slave states fought with the North. Some blacks, slave and free, voluntarily fought for the Confederacy.

History is infinitely more complex than demagogues, historically illiterate journalists and screenwriters try to make it.

Another lie repeated over and over is that Georgia changed its flag and that South Carolina raised its Confederate flag in defiance of the civil-rights movement. Not so. Airheads often think that whatever obsesses them obsesses everybody. Nevertheless there were other things going on in the 1960s besides the civil-rights movement. One was the centennial of the Civil War.

Georgia changed its flag in anticipation of the centennial, and South Carolina raised its flag during the centennial. Next to the American Revolution, no event is more significant in American history than the War. About 100,000 books have been written about it, and still more are being written about it. Tens of thousands of Americans visit the battlefields, collect memorabilia, participate in Civil War roundtables or in heritage organizations such as the Sons of Confederate Veterans and the Sons of the Veterans of the Grand Army of the Republic. Other thousands spend big sums on uniforms and equipment to re-enact the battles.

Trying to reduce interest in the Civil War to racism is nonsense.

Winston Churchill described the South's valiant fight against overwhelming odds as "one of the glorious moments in American history." That's what the Confederate flag symbolizes—the valor, honor and sacrifice of men who put their lives where their love of liberty was.

Anyone who wants to ban racist yahoos from waving the flag will get my help. They desecrate it. But if our Yankee high court won't let us protect the other flag we love, the American flag, it durn sure won't allow us to protect the Confederate flag.

We have more pressing problems to solve than to be quarreling over historic symbols. People who attack the Confederate symbols are racist and divisive. But trust me: As long as the flag is attacked, true Southerners will defend it. We will not allow our history and heritage to be made hostage to the ignorance and malice of others.

NOTES

[1] Drew Gilpin Faust, *"A Riddle of Death": Mortality and Meaning in the American Civil War* (Gettysburg, Penn.: Gettysburg College, 1995), 18.

[2] Dolly Blount Lamar, *When All Is Said and Done* (Athens: University of Georgia Press, 1952), 135.

[3] Almost all public monuments dedicated to individual soldiers during this period honor commissioned officers. Noteworthy exceptions include several Tennessee monuments to Sam Davis, who was hanged by the Union as a spy after refusing to name the friend who collaborated with him, and monuments in several towns to the earliest casualties of the war.

[4] Lewis I. Sharp, *John Quincy Adams Ward: Dean of American Sculpture* (Newark: University of Delaware Press, 1985), 175.

[5] Kirk Savage, *Standing Soldiers, Kneeling Slaves: Race, War, and Monument in Nineteenth-Century America* (Princeton, N.J.: Princeton University Press, 1997), 187.

[6] Millard F. Rogers Jr., *Randolph Rogers: American Sculptor in Rome* (Amherst: University of Massachusetts Press, 1971), 93.

[7] Peggy McDowell, "Martin Milmore's Soldiers' and Sailors' Monument on the Boston Common: Formulating Conventionalism in Design and Symbolism," *Journal of American Culture* 11 (1988): 65.

[8] Alfred S. Roe, *Monuments, Tablets, and Other Memorials Erected in Massachusetts to Commemorate the Service of Her Sons in the War of the Rebellion, 1861–1865* (Boston: Wright & Potter, 1910), 20.

[9] Minority Report of the Sub-Committee of Six, September 23, 1865, Miscellaneous Records of the Memorial Hall Committee of Fifty, Harvard University Archives.

[10] Frank Wheeler, "'Our Confederate Dead': The Story Behind Savannah's Confederate Monument," *Georgia Historical Quarterly* 82 (Summer 1998): 393.

[11] Dennis R. Montagna, "Henry Merwin Shrady's Ulysses S. Grant Memorial in Washington, D.C.: A Study in Iconography, Content and Patronage" (Ph.D. dissertation, University of Delaware, 1987), 144, 146–147.

[12] Michael Wilson Panhorst, "'Lest We Forget': Monuments and Memorial Sculpture in National Military Parks, 1861–1917" (Ph.D. dissertation, University of Delaware, 1988), 125.

[13] David M. Kahn, "The Grant Monument," *Journal of the Society of Architectural Historians* 41 (October 1982): 224.

[14] Gaines M. Foster, *Ghosts of the Confederacy: Defeat, the Lost Cause, and the Emergence of the New South* (New York: Oxford University Press, 1987), 132–33; Savage, *Standing Soldiers,* 176–77.

[15] Sabrina Shields Freeman, "Dan Rice's Monument: Patriotism or Circus Promotion?" *Pennsylvania Heritage* 12 (1986): 14.

[16] Changes in the siting of Confederate monuments reflected a related shift. Almost three-fourths of the monuments of known location installed before 1890 (not including memorial tablets, monuments placed in battlefield parks, or monuments to individuals unless specifically dedicated to a group) were placed in cemeteries. In the 1890s a majority of these monuments (55 percent) were not placed in cemeteries. That trend continued, and 86.5 percent of Confederate monuments dedicated during the years 1900 to 1919 were placed outside of cemeteries. Foster, *Ghosts of the Confederacy,* 40–41, 129, 158, reports similar statistics from a different data set.

[17] John Bodnar, *Remaking America: Public Memory, Commemoration, and Patriotism in the Twentieth Century* (Princeton, N.J.: Princeton University Press, 1992), 95.

[18] Sponsors of Confederate monuments also made this point through decisions about location. The promoters of the South Carolina Soldiers Monument in Columbia (1879) originally planned to place their statue in a cemetery or a city park, but upon the end of Reconstruction they decided to set it in front of the state house. A local newspaper declared that the choice "indicates the final recovery of South Carolina from the domination

of her enemies." John M. Bryan, *Creating the South Carolina State House* (Columbia: University of South Carolina Press, 1999), 90.

[19]David W. Blight, *Race and Reunion: The Civil War in American Memory* (Cambridge, Mass.: The Belknap Press of Harvard University Press, 2001), 90, 92, 94. Of course the decoration ritual itself expressed political statements. For example, by the 1890s blacks and whites held separate exercises at national cemeteries in the South. Ceremonies in the North remained integrated even though sponsoring GAR posts were generally segregated.

[20]Martha E. Kinney, "'If Vanquished I Am Still Victorious': Religious and Cultural Symbolism in Virginia's Confederate Memorial Day Celebrations, 1866–1930," *Virginia Magazine of History and Biography* 106 (Summer 1998): 264 n.64.

[21]Foster, *Ghosts of the Confederacy*, 134–35.

[22]Robert K. Sutton, ed., *Rally on the High Ground: The National Park Service Symposium on the Civil War, Ford's Theater, May 8 and 9, 2000* (Fort Washington, Penn.: Eastern National, 2001), v.

[23]Tony Horwitz, *Confederates in the Attic: Dispatches from the Unfinished Civil War* (New York: Pantheon Books, 1998), 126.

[24]Don Hinkle, *Embattled Banner: A Reasonable Defense of the Confederate Flag* (Paducah, Ky.: Turner Publishing Company, 1997), 61.

[25]Robert E. Bonner, *Colors & Blood: Flag Passions of the Confederate South* (Princeton, N.J.: Princeton University Press, 2002).

[26]John M. Coski, "The Confederate Battle Flag in Historical Perspective," in *Confederate Symbols in the Contemporary South,* edited by J. Michael Martinez, William D. Richardson, and Ron McNinch-Su (Gainesville: University Press of Florida, 2000), 89–129.

2
Women of the War

Commemoration of Union and Confederate women differed much more sharply than commemoration of Union and Confederate soldiers. Public remembrance of northern women declined steadily in the years after the war. In contrast, recognition of white southern women was a vital element of the culture of the Lost Cause. Reworked in the 1930s, the theme took a lasting place at the center of American popular culture.

This disparity is in some ways puzzling. Prescriptive wartime literature in the North and the South urged women to assume similar roles that were based on deeply rooted conceptions of warfare as a gender-defining activity in which women encouraged, rewarded, and comforted male combatants. Men and women on both sides recognized that homefront contributions to morale would be especially critical in a war between two democracies relying primarily on volunteer soldiers, and both sides paid tribute to women during the war for sacrificing their sons, husbands, and brothers—and in many ways their own lives—for the cause. Moreover, on both sides the strains of the war not only reinforced traditional gender roles but also brought women into new activities. Initiatives like the Union and Confederate recruitment of women nurses introduced potentially transformative gender images that conservatives sought to contain.

Like the shared ideas about women's role in war, several of the distinctive wartime experiences of Confederate women do not provide a simple explanation for the contrasting patterns of remembrance in North and South. White southern women saw a higher proportion of their men leave for the war and a lower proportion return from it, but these statistics alone do not account for the commemorative prominence of white southern women, for the South did not outpace the North in honoring volunteers and fallen soldiers as it did in honoring women who supported those volunteers and mourned the dead. To be sure, the conduct of Confederate women in direct encounters with Union soldiers was an important part of southern remembrance, but that experience was not highlighted in formal commemorations like public monuments. Instead, southern monuments routinely praised women for ministering to wounded soldiers, although white southern women were comparatively hesitant to work as nurses. Most often monuments celebrated the steadfast patriotism of Confederate women, notwithstanding the antiwar sentiments they expressed as the Confederacy collapsed.

The neglect of Union women and veneration of Confederate women undoubtedly did reflect some sectional differences in wartime experiences, particularly the northern experience of victory and the southern experience of defeat. The commemorative gulf also reflected variations within a national debate over the emergence of the so-called "New Woman" after the war. Northern women accounted for much of the memory of Union women, which often resonated with feminist themes. Northern men, southern men, and southern women all took strong interests in remembrance of Confederate women, whose image became more vigorously disputed. The understanding of white southern women's Civil War as a negotiation between the pull of tradition and the forces of change was a powerful framework of memory that would adapt readily to a broader vision of modern womanhood.

UNION WOMEN

During the Civil War, northerners routinely recognized women as active participants in the conflict. Widely circulated literature and print images lauded women for sustaining the willpower of men while enduring the emotional ordeal of the war. Perhaps the best-remembered of the many tributes to Union women's patriotism is John Greenleaf Whittier's popular ballad "Barbara Freitchie" (1863), the story of an elderly woman who supposedly defied Stonewall Jackson by flying the American flag from her house in the temporarily occupied town of Frederick, Maryland. Women's activities in soldiers' aid societies and as nurses also received considerable attention during the war and prompted two large tribute volumes immediately afterward: Frank Moore's *Women of the War: Their Heroism and Self-Sacrifice* (1866) and Linus P. Brockett and Mary C. Vaughan's *Women's Work in the Civil War: A Record of Heroism, Patriotism, and Patience* (1867). Louisa May Alcott's successful fictional treatment of her month as a Union nurse, *Hospital Sketches* (1863), provided a springboard for a literary career that would include publication of the most enduring saga of the northern homefront, *Little Women* (1868–69). The interest in Union nurses connected women of the war not only with domesticity but also with an expansion of opportunities for female adventure. Sara Emma Edmonds's fictionalized account of her battlefield experiences dressed as a man, *Nurse and Spy* (1864), sold an estimated 175,000 copies.[1]

This recognition of the importance of Union women did not long outlast the war. The popular magazines *Century* and *McClure's* published more than 120 articles and reminiscences about the Civil War between 1887 and 1900, none of which focused on the experiences of northern women. *McClure's, Harper's Weekly,* and *Ladies' Home Journal* published a total of four stories about wartime northern women during the years 1880 to 1900. Much more common were works of fiction about the wartime experiences of white southern women and intersectional reconciliation romances that featured white southern women. *Harper's* and *Harper's Weekly* published twelve reunion stories with southern heroines after 1880 but only two with northern heroines.[2] Clyde Fitch's play *Barbara Freitchie* (1899) even recast Whittier's personification of Union women's patriotism as a young Confederate. Union women were similarly absent from the Civil War commemorative landscape. A memorial tablet in Auburn, New York (1914), was the only monument to the remarkable adventures of Harriet Tubman as a scout, spy, and guide. Nor did northerners salute the more conventional wartime virtues of women by putting up monuments that saluted women for maintaining the morale and sharing the sacrifices of the victorious side. Confederate soldiers monuments with inscriptions recognizing women were more than three times as numerous as the parallel Union monuments.

Contests over the image of the Union nurse were among the most revealing aspects of the remembrance of northern women. Ideas about Civil War nursing developed in the shadow of cultural expectations shaped by conventional gender roles and by the specific precedent of Florence Nightingale, whose work a few years earlier in the Crimean War had made her one of the most famous women in the world.

Commemoration of Union nurses tended to highlight women like Nightingale who were not affiliated with the government and who established themselves as direct representatives of homefront sentiment, such as Mary Ann "Mother" Bickerdyke, the so-called Cyclone in Calico of the western theater; Clara Barton, who worked near the front lines in the East; and the women who served on hospital transport ships organized by the U.S. Sanitary Commission. These women did not have quite the elite class standing of Nightingale but were mostly from the middle classes or higher. In contrast, the women nurses paid by the United States came from a wider range of class backgrounds and faced more grueling day-to-day negotiations over their status as hospital workers, including endless confrontations with physicians who claimed full authority over hospitals.

The tension between the two models was reflected in the decline in the reputation of Dorothea Dix, who was appointed Superintendent of Women Nurses because her tireless crusade for the establishment of state mental hospitals had made her an exemplar of antebellum middle-class women's benevolence. Ambivalent about the initiative in women's paid labor that she headed, Dix downplayed the affiliation of her office with the federal government. Conflicts not only with army doctors but also with free-lance nurses whose voluntaristic ethos she shared and with U.S. Sanitary Commission leaders eager to integrate relief efforts with the federal bureaucracy caused Dix to be regarded widely as a failure. Had she challenged that assessment, she might have substantially enhanced remembrance of the Office of Women Nurses, but she avoided commemoration of wartime nursing. Elected president for life of the Army Nurses Association, she ignored the organization for the most part and opposed its calls for pensions and women's suffrage.[3]

Dix's reticence was especially significant because northern women were responsible for much of the remembrance of northern women's efforts during the war. Former nurses wrote more than a score of narratives about their experiences, retracing the conflicts with doctors and among nurses but also fostering a community of memory. Often isolated from other women during the war, Clara Barton celebrated both government and unaffiliated nurses as her co-workers in her widely circulated poem "The Women Who Went to the Field" (1892), though the American Red Cross founder sighed that memory of those women was "fast fading away." Similarly, northern women sponsored the major civic monuments to Union nurses. The Women's Relief Corps commissioned Theo Alice Ruggles Kitson to model the monument to Mary Bickerdyke in Galesburg, Illinois (1906). The state chapter of the Daughters of Union Veterans donated the Army Nurses Memorial installed in the Massachusetts state house in 1911. And president Ellen Jolly led the Ladies' Auxiliary of the Ancient Order of Hibernians in overcoming the initial resistance of the War Department to a monument in Washington to Catholic nuns who served as nurses, which was dedicated in 1924. Through their sponsorship and their focus on nurses rather than all Union women, these monuments tended to envision nursing as a realm of women's leadership rather than as an example of instinctual female benevolence and support for men.

The most ambitious attempt to commemorate Union women only partly succeeded in expressing the same theme. Coordinated by Mabel A. Boardman, successor to Clara Barton as the leader of the American Red Cross, this initiative asked Congress in 1912 for an appropriation of $400,000, to be matched by private donations in the name of the New York chapter of the Military Order of the Loyal Legion, for a national headquarters in Washington that would serve as a memorial to the wartime work of Union women. After southerners objected that the Red Cross "belongs as much to the South as to the North," the project was converted into a memorial to the Civil War women of both sections, and the Loyal Legion was dropped as a source of matching funds.[4] The cornerstone-laying ceremonies in March 1915 and dedication in May 1917 showed that the splendid building would do little to honor Union women. The orators did not mention Barton's achievements in the Civil War or draw more general connections between Union women's activities and the work of the Red Cross, as Barton had in "The Women Who Went to the Field." Instead, Senator John Sharp Williams of Mississippi delivered a robust tribute at the dedication to the steadfast white women who had inspired the armies of the South. Even at the site designed to recognize them most grandly in the civic landscape, Union women did not receive as much attention as Confederate women.

8

CLARA BARTON

Account of a Public Lecture

1882

The emergence of Barton (1821–1912) as the leading Union heroine of the war did not result solely from the drama of her work nursing near battlefields and the poignancy of her efforts after the war to find missing soldiers, which involved her in the emotionally charged plight of prisoners of war and led her to play a prominent role in the establishment of a cemetery for the 13,000 Union dead at Andersonville prison. Her reputation also grew out of the popularity of the public lectures in which she recounted these experiences. Like most nurses' recollections, her lectures expressed a deep admiration for rank-and-file soldiers, and veterans avidly enjoyed the presentations. This reminiscence describes a lecture sponsored by a veterans group that was unaware that Barton had repeatedly, if somewhat circumspectly, expressed support for the women's rights movement after the war. What do the veterans' assumptions and Barton's response indicate about the ways in which different sets of northerners envisioned Union nurses?

The [news]papers of the day were passed to me for inspection. After arraying me in sufficiently gorgeous mental and moral attire, ascribing to me all the virtuous qualities I had not, they had completed their peroration with the following comforting assurance:

> We can promise our citizens a rare treat of patriotic eloquence such as is seldom listened to and we can assure them that there will be no cause for disappointment. They will not have thrust upon them a lecture on woman's rights after the style of Susan B. Anthony and her clique.* Miss Barton does not belong to that class of women.

*Susan B. Anthony (1820–1906) and Elizabeth Cady Stanton (1815–1902) were leaders of the woman suffrage movement.

Clara Barton Papers, Library of Congress.

My blood boiled as I read and faced an audience of which the most exacting speaker might be proud, not even standing room in the aisles. And I treated them to their feast of "Patriotic eloquence" [with] a vim I had no power to control. I could feel the indignation hiss between my teeth as the words rolled almost unbidden, but I held firmly to my subject till it was ended, and when they had shouted and cheered to a tiger I resumed — in the following text —

"Soldiers, you have called me here to speak to you on the war we lived together. I have done it. Now I have a word for you. I wish to read this paragraph which you have used to help fill your hall." I read it very slowly and distinctly.

"That paragraph, my comrades, does worse than misrepresent me as a woman, it maligns my friend and it [disparages] the brightest and bravest work ever done in this land for either me or you. You glorify the women who made their way to the front to seek you out in your misery and nurse you back to life. You call us angels. Who opened the way for us to go, and made it possible, who but that detested set of women who for years had claimed that women had rights and should have the privilege to exercise them, the right to her own property, her own children, her own home, to her freedom of action, to her personal liberty, and upon this other women claimed the right and took the courage if only to go to a camp and drag a wounded man out of a swamp and try to save him for his family and his country.

"And soldiers, for every woman's hand that ever cooled your fevered brow, staunched your bleeding wounds or called life back to your famished body you should bless God for Susan B. Anthony, Cady Stanton and their followers. No one has stood so alone, so unhelped as Susan Anthony, and Soldiers I would have the first monument that is ever raised to any woman in this country raised to her, and that monument will be raised and your daughters, boys, will help proudly, gratefully help to set its granite blocks for everlasting age, set it where all may see. . . .

"Boys, three cheers for Susan B. Anthony!"
And the very windows shook in their casements.

CONFEDERATE WOMEN

Wartime commemoration identified patriotism as the new heart of white southern womanhood. The most famous depiction of this theme developed from an incident in the Peninsula campaign of 1862. Upon learning that a group of white southern women, assisted by slaves, had provided a funeral and burial for Lieutenant William Latané, the only Confederate casualty in General J. E. B. Stuart's daring ride around the Union lines, Richmond author John R. Thompson published a poem about the event that achieved wide circulation as a broadside. Virginia painter William D. Washington's 1864 rendition of the subject proved immensely popular in its initial studio exhibition and was subsequently displayed at the state capitol, where a bucket was placed beneath the canvas for donations to the cause. A. G. Campbell's print version of the image (Figure 2-1) would soon become one of the most popular icons of Confederate remembrance.

The celebration of white women as embodiments of Confederate sentiment persisted after the war. "The soldiers have abandoned the fight, and only the women continue it," maintained a southern belle in John W. DeForest's novel *The Bloody Chasm* (1881), one of many works of fiction and drama in which a level-headed Union veteran won the affections of a passionate rebel.[5] DeForest, who had published several books before serving as an officer in a Connecticut infantry regiment, updated the conciliatory intersectional romances of the 1850s to create this formula with his *Miss Ravenel's Conversion From Secession to Loyalty* (1867), which was imitated widely in the 1880s and 1890s. Northern men wrote many of the reunion romances, but Virginia author Thomas Nelson Page and other white southern men also eagerly burnished white southern women's reputation for extraordinary attachment to the Confederacy.

Women took an active part in the development of their political identity, often stressing the individual autonomy that was a precondition to their reputation for loyalty. The heroine of Augusta Jane Evans's wartime bestseller *Macaria; or Altars of Sacrifice* (1864) forswore marriage to care for wounded Confederate soldiers and establish an orphanage for their children. The adventures of celebrated Confederate spy Belle Boyd offered a model of womanhood in which patriotism led to excitement through skillful manipulation of gender identity. Novels written by white southern women in the twenty years after the war sometimes demonstrated considerably more autonomy than Confederate loyalty, using the formula of the intersectional romance to criticize tendencies of white southern men.[6]

The tensions between deference and citizenship in the image of Confederate women took on a new intensity when the woman suffrage

Figure 2-1. A. G. Campbell, after William D. Washington, *The Burial of Latané,* **1868 engraving of 1864 painting.** Why did this image become one of the most popular icons of the Confederacy?

The Museum of the Confederacy, Richmond, Virginia. Photograph by Katherine Wetzel.

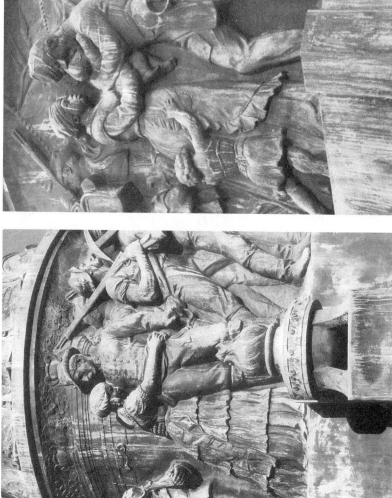

Figure 2-2. Moses Ezekiel, *Confederate Monument*, Arlington National Cemetery, 1914 (Details). Why does this monument highlight the moment at which soldiers take leave of women?

Photos by Thomas Brown.

movement accelerated in the last decade of the nineteenth century. Suffrage opponents argued that the movement betrayed the legacy of the Confederacy. Mildred Lewis Rutherford, president of the Georgia division of the United Daughters of the Confederacy (UDC), declared that "the women who are working for this measure are striking at the principle for which their fathers fought during the Civil War. Woman's suffrage comes from the North and West and from women who do not believe in state's rights and who wish to see negro women using the ballot."[7] Some reformers did seek to throw off the legacy of the Lost Cause. "Men of the Old South, armed with all the implements of war, and supplied with the wealth of states, fought for empire based on slavery, and lost," declared one southern woman in 1895. "The women of the New South, armed with clear-cut, unanswerable argument alone, are struggling for liberty based on justice, and will win."[8] But other supporters envisioned suffrage as an extension, rather than a repudiation, of the political position white southern women had developed through their support of the Confederacy. Prominent southern suffragists Rebecca Latimer Felton, Belle Kearney, and Nellie Nugent Somerville were all members of the UDC.

At this important juncture, public monuments took up the theme of Confederate women. Many soldiers monuments already acknowledged the postwar loyalty of white southern women by identifying them as the sponsors of the memorials. To this recognition was added commemoration of women's wartime efforts. Soldiers monuments saluted Confederate women either in separate inscriptions or, in some cases, as part of the main inscription. McDuffie County, Georgia (ca. 1911), even gave women top billing in a monument dedicated "IN MEMORY OF / THE WOMEN OF THE SIXTIES / AND THE CONFEDERATE SOLDIERS." Other soldiers monuments did not mention women in their inscriptions but centered their designs on the partnership between Confederate men and women. Moses Ezekiel's circular frieze on the Confederate monument at Arlington National Cemetery (1914) depicted four different male-female pairs at the departure for war, including scenes of volunteers leaving behind a wife, a mother, and a slave mammy (Figure 2-2).

In addition to assuming a place alongside soldiers on monuments, Confederate women became a subject for separate monuments. Sponsorship of these monuments differed from fund-raising for soldiers monuments, as men played a more prominent role. White southern women did contribute significantly to the commemoration. The members assembled tribute books like *South Carolina Women in the Confederacy* (1903) and sponsored a few monuments, such as the memorial erected in Gadsden, Alabama, in 1907 to Emma Sansom, the teenager celebrated for helping General Nathan Bedford Forrest's army to a victory by leading him to a ford across a creek after Union forces had destroyed the bridge. But the larger projects generally represented themselves as the initiatives of men. Rarely did these efforts involve a wide solicitation of contributions, and as a result, the monuments tended to rely on state funding or the donations of a small group of patrons.

The monuments depicted several activities as characteristic of Confederate women. Statuary groups of women reading histories of the war to children in Raleigh, North Carolina (1914), and Jacksonville, Florida (1916), honored white southern women's work of remembrance and motherhood. The Arkansas Monument to Confederate Women (1913) portrayed a woman's farewell to her son as he left for the war. Images of women tending to wounded soldiers appeared on many of the women's monuments and also as subordinate relief panels on monuments dedicated jointly to Confederate men and women in Raymond (1908) and Greenwood (1913), Mississippi. Several works represented women praying, and one veteran proposed that the ideal monument would reproduce *The Burial of Latané* because "it was in her divine, angelic nature that the Southern woman appeared in her most conspicuous refulgence, and with the Bible she was far more potent and useful than in all other ways during the war."[9]

Two recurrent themes in Confederate women's monuments illustrated the contradictory tendencies in these representations. Many works depicted a woman holding a flag, which reinforced the image of the white southern woman as an embodiment of Confederate political identity. On the other hand, the frieze at Arlington National Cemetery was not alone in suggesting that the model Confederate woman might be a slave. A former Confederate chaplain delivering an address in which he imagined a sculptor depicting "the virtues of the Southern women of 1861" began with a figure of a slave mammy and declared that "the monument to the Southern woman will be a monument to our faithful old Dinahs and Delias too."[10] The UDC campaigned for a national mammy memorial in Washington, D.C., which the Senate approved in 1923 with an appropriation of $200,000, but the measure failed in the House of Representatives.

The long campaign to place a monument to Confederate women on the grounds of every state capitol in the South provided the fullest discussion of the various commemorative strategies. Launched in 1895, the undertaking was noteworthy in part for two goals that were not realized. Supporters sought to commission multiple copies of the same monument to women, partly to save money but also to "demonstrate that the entire South, together as a whole, not separate communities, united in paying this grand tribute."[11] This appeal differed sharply from the pattern of soldiers monuments, in which community leaders strived to emphasize the unique local features even of mass-produced works. Advocates of the monument also faced strong arguments from women that a more useful form of commemoration would be more appropriate. Women suggested the endowment of a retirement home, a college, a scholarship fund, and a boardinghouse for southern women studying in New York City. General C. Irvine Walker, the veteran leading the campaign, expressed regret that such proposals would be too expensive, but the veterans clearly preferred a monument to a utilitarian memorial of the same cost.

Walker's monument committee ignited a controversy in 1909 when it selected a design submitted by the sculptor Louis Amateis (Figure 2-3). Like the Confederate monuments he had designed for Houston (1908), Corsicana (1909), and Galveston (1912), Texas, Amateis's proposal for the women's monument was an energetic composition. The treasurer of the campaign for a Confederate monument at Arlington National Cemetery endorsed it as expressing "the unconquerable spirit, the dauntless courage, the unfailing devotion, which animated the women of the Confederacy." But *Confederate Veteran* editor Sumner Cunningham argued that "monuments of this design would certainly reflect so seriously upon the divine qualities of southern womanhood that if they were furnished free there would be serious objection to exposing them to public view."[12] Minister H. M. Hamill wrote that "it violates every canon of art or good taste or historic condition." (See Document 9.)

After veterans almost unanimously rejected Amateis's design at the 1909 annual meeting, Walker's committee turned to a proposal by Belle Kinney, the daughter of a Tennessee veteran. Her model depicted a

The Women of the Southern Confederacy

Figure 2-3. Louis Amateis, *Drawing of Proposed Monument to Confederate Women,* **1909.** How did responses to this image reveal conflicting ideas about the legacy of Confederate women?

Reprinted from *Confederate Veteran* 17 (April 1909): 150. Courtesy of the University of South Carolina.

young Confederate woman unconsciously crowned by Fame while she places a palm leaf on a dying soldier (Figure 2-4). The work received considerable praise but also some sharp criticism. Mrs. George H. Tichenor of New Orleans, whose husband had initiated the women's monument campaign in 1895, strenuously lobbied the UDC to protest against adoption of Kinney's design. She maintained that the work "gives an utterly false idea of the Women of the War," for the war "was a period that called for immediate action, not for timid shrinking and fearfulness of spirit. Our mothers met the call of the hour courageously, undauntedly, and when Appomattox came faced defeat as proudly as once they exulted in success." She argued that Kinney's design "has singled out one feature, Appomattox alone, wholly ignoring the long, brave days of selfless loving endeavor," making it "singularly weak and unrepresentative of the story it effects to commemorate." The UDC pronounced itself "unwilling to endorse the design."[13] Kinney modified her composition, perhaps in response to the criticisms, and the revised version was adopted for the Mississippi and Tennessee monuments to Confederate women (Figure 2-5).

Around the time of the dedication of the Nashville monument in late 1926, twenty-six-year-old Atlanta writer Margaret Mitchell began work on what would become the most influential "monument" to white southern women of the Civil War era. A sensation on its publication in June 1936, *Gone With the Wind* sold a million copies in the first six months and twenty-five million more copies over the next fifty years.[14] The film adaptation that opened in Atlanta in December 1939 immediately became one of the best-known movies in history.

Gone With the Wind had a complicated relationship with the commemoration of Confederate women on which it built. The epic updated and leveraged the oft-rehearsed theme that women's struggles on the homefront were at least as important as the battles in which men fought. Indifferent to politics and disdainful of self-sacrifice, protagonist Scarlett O'Hara largely rejected the competing models of Confederate womanhood advanced by Amateis and Kinney. At the same time, Scarlett's ambivalent pursuit of a different strategy of womanhood followed precedent in connecting gender ideals to hierarchies of race and class, and the work treated with considerable sympathy a major character squarely in the tradition of the Confederate heroine,

Figure 2-4. **Belle Kinney,** *Model of Proposed Monument to Confederate Women,* **1909–1910.** What are the characteristics of Kinney's ideal Confederate woman?

Reprinted from *Confederate Veteran* 18 (March 1910): 97. Courtesy of the University of South Carolina.

Figure 2-5 (*opposite*). **Belle Kinney,** *Mississippi Monument to Confederate Women,* **Jackson, 1909–1912.** Did Kinney's final version respond to the criticisms of her initial design?

Photo courtesy of Mississippi Department of Archives and History.

Melanie Hamilton. Most important, *Gone With the Wind* mirrored previous commemorations by presenting the Civil War as an event that simultaneously opened new lives for white southern women and deepened their ties to an old order.

Approaching the seventy-fifth anniversary of publication, *Gone With the Wind* remains a living — and sharply contested — presence in American culture. Its enduring popularity sustains a market for collectibles, tourism, publications, and films that would have gratified the grandest material ambitions of Scarlett O'Hara, and many readers and viewers continue to find her example meaningful in their lives. It also inspires numerous parodies, including male drag performances that literary scholar Elizabeth Young has described as apt epitomes of "the character's combination of hyperbolic femininity and symbolic masculinity."[15] And it has drawn vigorous criticism in many forms, asking why the racial perspective of *Gone With the Wind* has not caused it to be repudiated by white popular culture. Beloved, deplored, and frequently reimagined, the white southern woman of the Civil War provides an important illustration of the crosscurrents of American memory.

9

HOWARD M. HAMILL

Confederate Woman's Monument

April 1909

Hamill (1847–1915) was a Methodist clergymen and served as chaplain general of the United Confederate Veterans. This letter to *Confederate Veteran* details the objections frequently expressed in that magazine to Louis Amateis's design for a monument to Confederate women (Figure 2-3). What does he dislike about the image?

H. M. Hamill, "Confederate Woman's Monument," *Confederate Veteran* 17 (April 1909): 150.

I was a boy under Lee in his hardest fighting division the last year of the war. I wear with pride my bronze veteran's cross, the gift of the U.D.C. My mother was a Confederate woman, and therefore of that worthy company whom the "Confederate woman's monument" is designed to honor. I can well remember her tireless service at sewing, nursing, cooking, and other loving ministry to sick and wounded Confederates, and how her brown hair grew gray and health failed under her self-imposed burden during those dark days of war. I trust this will be my warrant for timely criticism of the proposed woman's monument as recently pictured in newspapers and exploited as the accepted symbol of the women of the Confederacy. I first saw the design a week ago as I sat with some ladies in a Florida train, and I think I express the judgment of both women and men when I condemn it. It violates every canon of art or good taste or historic condition. In brief, it presents the typical woman of the Confederacy standing in defiant pose upon a pedestal something after the manner of that other "I Will" Chicago travesty in symbolism that confronted Exposition visitors* except that this brawny Southern Amazon in her right hand is brandishing an antique sword which she grips by the blade and not by the hilt! Beneath her feet, as the text of a stump speech which she is artistically supposed to be making, is carved the sentence, "Uphold Our State Rights."

Not a line of womanly grace or modesty or tenderness, not a hint of the dear home keeper and home builder of the Southland, not a reminder of the sweet and gentle minister of mercy and comfort who bent over the hospital cot and soothed the pain of the wounded soldier and left in his heart of gratitude forever a true picture of that noblest of all memories of the Confederacy, the patient, self-sacrificing, unwearied helper and comforter of the boys in gray. Nor is there a hint in the unsightly figure proposed of those thousands of heroic souls who in loneliness and dread of evil tidings from the front took care of the absent soldiers' home, kept in order the servants, taught the children, made lint of their cherished linens for the army surgeon, brewed home medicines for the sick, watched after the growing crops, wrote brave letters to the front when their own hearts were breaking, and thus won imperishable love and honor from every soldier in gray down to the latest of his descendants. Think of the sweet little home body of the Southland, brandishing a big sword by the blade and declaiming like a candidate for the Legislature an oration upon State rights!

No, I am not an artist, but I think I know a work of art when I see it, and I am tolerably sure that the Confederate woman does not care to be reincarnated in bronze as a composite of the classic Amazon, the

*Hamill refers to Daniel Chester French's allegorical statue *The Republic* at the Columbian Exposition of 1893.

Wagnerian Brunehilda, and Carrie Nation!* That old picture of the Carthaginian women weaving the strands of their hair into bowstrings for husbands and sons or of Cornelia pointing to her children as her jewels or even the little brown mothers of Japan twisting their braids into a mighty rope to sound the temple bell have more art and beauty and pathos and truth to me than this besworded symbol of a kind of Southern woman that never existed and I pray never may exist save in this artist's fancy.

*Brunhild, whose name means "fighter in armor," is a queen of Iceland in the opera cycle that Richard Wagner based on the Nibelungenlied. Carrie Nation (1846–1922) was a temperance agitator famous for raiding saloons with a hatchet.

10

LAURA MARTIN ROSE

Address on Dedication of Mississippi Monument to Confederate Women

June 3, 1912

Later historian-general of the UDC, Rose (1862–1917) was president of the Mississippi division when she delivered this address at a state UDC meeting held in conjunction with the unveiling of the monument in Jackson to women of the Confederacy. Although Belle Kinney's work depicted a young Confederate woman, Rose's address is typical in its emphasis on mothers as the most important exemplars of Confederate womanhood. How else does she describe the typical Confederate woman? In what ways is her address similar to and different from Hamill's vision of Confederate women?

We are assembled to-day to memorialize the sublime sacrifices and unparalleled love and devotion of that noble band, the women of the Confederacy. Far from the noise and din of battle, "with no marshaling troops, no bivouac song, no banners to gleam and wave," these grand Southern women waged a battle greater than any fought on land or sea.

"Address of Mrs. S. E. F. Rose at Jackson," *Confederate Veteran* 20 (September 1912): 413–14.

One of the proudest memories of the War of the States is the conduct of the women of the Confederacy, who willingly gave their all—fathers, husbands, sons, and brothers—to the service of the Confederacy. With no thought of self, at the first call to arms in '61 they bade their protectors Godspeed and undertook the support of their families, aged parents, and children. They deprived themselves of even the necessities of life in order to care for the sick and wounded soldiers and feed and clothe all those within their reach. There were no idle moments in those Southern homes. The women were constantly spinning, knitting, and weaving to provide garments for those in the army and struggling to carry on their home affairs.

These women, reared in luxury, unused to aught but indoor employments such as the customs of the country assigned to women, in the absence of the men, all of whom were at the front, planted, cultivated, and gathered the crops, chopped and hauled wood, and fed and attended to the stock, cheerfully performing such duties as their part of the sacrifices necessary to achieve the independence of the Confederacy.

The heroism of these noble women was a moral heroism even greater and grander than that of the soldiers who fell in the excitement of battle. We hear heralded throughout the world the courage of the Spartan mother who urged her sons to go to battle and return with their shields or upon them. We are proud to say that heroism did not die with the ancients, for the women of the Confederacy gave to the world an exhibition of bravery and unselfish devotion never excelled and rarely equaled in all history. Many instances of her courage could be related; one, although often told, will be given again. Governor Letcher, war Governor of Virginia, returning from a visit to his home at Staunton, stopped at the house of an old friend. The good woman of the house was alone, and she told the Governor that her husband, father, and ten sons were all in the same company in the army. "You must be very lonely," the Governor said, "accustomed to so large a family." "Yes," this noble matron replied, "it is hard to be alone; but if I had ten more sons, they should all be in the army."

Is it any wonder that with such mothers the Confederate soldiers for four years, although far outnumbered, poorly equipped, almost starved, and often barefooted, thrilled the world with their deeds of courage and daring? Never before in the annals of history did so many brave and patriotic men with such a unanimity of purpose rally around a common standard from purely patriotic motives.

The great Napoleon on being asked what was the greatest need of his country replied, "Mothers." The South had mothers, and these same mothers furnished to the world the Confederate soldier, whose courage has never been equaled in the world's history. These mothers transmitted to their sons this courage of adamant and devotion to principle....

NOTES

[1]Lyde Cullen Sizer, *The Political Work of Northern Women Writers and the Civil War, 1850–1872* (Chapel Hill: University of North Carolina Press, 2000), 179.

[2]Alice Fahs, "The Feminized Civil War: Gender, Northern Popular Literature, and the Memory of the War, 1861–1900," *Journal of American History* 85 (March 1999): 1491. Romances of reunion that featured northern heroines, such as Henry James's *The Bostonians* (1886), Thomas Nelson Page's *Red Rock* (1898), Owen Wister's *The Virginian* (1902), and Thomas Dixon's *The Clansman* (1905) frequently lamented the postwar emergence of the so-called New Woman in the North and featured plots in which a politically assertive northern woman accepted subordination to a southern man.

[3]Thomas J. Brown, *Dorothea Dix, New England Reformer* (Cambridge, Mass.: Harvard University Press, 1998), 274–323.

[4]*Congressional Record,* 62d Cong., 2d sess. (August 12, 1912).

[5]Nina Silber, *The Romance of Reunion: Northerners and the South, 1865–1900* (Chapel Hill: University of North Carolina Press, 1993), 111.

[6]Drew Gilpin Faust, *Mothers of Invention: Women of the Slaveholding South in the American Civil War* (Chapel Hill: University of North Carolina Press, 1996); Jane Turner Censer, "Reimagining the North-South Reunion: Southern Women Novelists and the Intersectional Romance, 1876–1900," *Southern Cultures* 5 (Summer 1999): 64–91.

[7]Marjorie Spruill Wheeler, *New Women of the New South: The Leaders of the Woman Suffrage Movement in the Southern States* (New York: Oxford University Press, 1993), 25.

[8]Josephine K. Henry, "The New Women of the New South," *Arena* 11 (February 1895): 357.

[9]J. E. Deupree, "Southern Woman's Monument," *Confederate Veteran* 17 (July 1909): 362.

[10]John Levi Underwood, *The Women of the Confederacy* (New York: The Neale Publishing Co., 1906), 56, 60.

[11]"Memorial to Women of the Confederacy," *Confederate Veteran* 14 (October 1906): 462.

[12]Wallace Streater, "Favors Design," *Confederate Veteran* 17 (June 1909): 205; "Monument to Confederate Women," *Confederate Veteran* 17 (April 1909): 152.

[13]Elise L. Smith, "Belle Kinney and the Confederate Women's Monument," *Southern Quarterly* 32 (Summer 1994): 19.

[14]Helen Taylor, *Scarlett's Women:* Gone With the Wind *and Its Female Fans* (New Brunswick, N.J.: Rutgers University Press, 1989), 1–2.

[15]Elizabeth Young, *Disarming the Nation: Women's Writing and the American Civil War* (Chicago: University of Chicago Press, 1999), 281.

3

Robert E. Lee and the Lost Cause

Commemoration of the Confederacy has featured not only rank-and-file soldiers and loyal women of the homefront but also a gallery of individual heroes. Though highly controversial during the war, Jefferson Davis emerged as a symbol of the white southern ordeal through his postwar imprisonment and enjoyed great regional popularity long after his death in 1889. Generations of white southerners recounted the exploits of dashing cavalrymen like J. E. B. Stuart, Turner Ashby, and "the Gray Ghost," John Singleton Mosby. By far the most important figure in postwar imagination of the Confederacy has been General Robert E. Lee. For southerners and northerners alike, his experience has served as one of the main vehicles for remembering the war as a coherent narrative from secession to reunion, charged with political lessons for society and moral guidance for ordinary individuals.

Several different phases of Lee's career have figured prominently in Civil War commemoration. The position of his family in a Virginia elite dating back to the colonial period and his close ties to the family of George Washington have often caused Lee to be regarded as representative of the social order of the Old South. His decisions to decline a command in the United States Army and accept a commission in the Confederacy have frequently been treated as a miniature of the entire process of disunion. His battles have been relived countless times. His surrender at Appomattox and postwar tenure as president of Washington College in Lexington, Virginia, have provided measures of white southern willingness to accept defeat and rebuild the region. Each of these themes has inspired a variety of commemorations, and the choice of emphasis among them has often had significant implications. For example, ex-Confederates disdainful of sectional reconciliation preferred to recall Lee's military prowess rather than his surrender.

Postwar arguments over the direction of the South illustrated the magic of Lee's name in the region. Confederate veteran George Washington Cable's famous essay "The Silent South" (1885), which called on southern whites to reform the repressive racial order, opened with a long description of the towering Lee Monument unveiled in New Orleans one year earlier. Cable observed that "this monument, lifted far above our daily strife of narrow interests and often narrower passions and misunderstandings, becomes a monument to more than its one great and rightly loved original. It symbolizes our whole South's better self; that finer part which the world not always sees."[1] But if Lee was for Cable an emblem of the potential for progressivism in the South, he was also a hero of the reactionary forces that soon drove Cable from his home region because of his challenge to white supremacism.

Northerners, too, have regarded Lee as an important symbol and debated the proper attitude toward him. The most dramatic illustration of northern ambivalence has been the treatment of Lee's antebellum home, Arlington, across the Potomac River from Washington, D.C. Occupied by Union troops at the outset of the war, Arlington became the property of the United States after the owner, Lee's wife, failed to deliver a tax payment required by the Direct Tax Act of 1862. In June 1864, Quartermaster General Montgomery C. Meigs ordered the burial of Union dead at the estate, beginning in the rose garden next to the mansion. By the end of the war, the United States had vividly laid responsibility for thousands of deaths at Lee's doorstep. Although Arlington National Cemetery was thus founded in denunciation of Lee, Arlington would become a federal shrine to him sixty years later with the establishment of the Lee Mansion National Memorial.

Such national tributes to Lee offer an opportunity to evaluate the stability of the commemorative culture of sectional reconciliation that matured in the early twentieth century. The late twentieth century saw a reinvigoration of protests characterizing veneration for the Confederate commander as contrary to fundamental principles of the United States. Conversely, a vein of white southern remembrance continued to resist national claims on the Confederate image. The remarkable transition from a regional to a national hero that made Lee an American icon in the years after 1900 threatened to leave him with neither base of support a century later.

SOUTHERN HERO

Lee's emergence as the preeminent hero of the postwar South requires some explanation. Some scholars have argued that Stonewall Jackson was more popular until his death in May 1863 and suggested that the relentless, pious, and eccentric commander from the mountains appealed more to the wartime values of white southerners than the Cavalier image personified by Lee. Moreover, Jackson's accidental death at the zenith of Confederate military fortunes invited white southerners to speculate wishfully about what might have happened if he had lived. Lee, in contrast, had led his army to defeat.

Yet Lee was clearly first in the hearts of white southerners in the decades after the war. Jackson figured prominently in Confederate commemoration, as evidenced by the statues of him unveiled in Baltimore, Maryland (1870); Richmond, Virginia (1875); and New Orleans, Louisiana (1881). To a remarkable extent, however, Lee's reputation absorbed the fame of his former lieutenant. Printmakers came to represent Jackson's death primarily through images of a mourning Lee. Also popular were depictions of the generals' last meeting at Chancellorsville. Everett B. D. Julio's 1869 painting of this event (Figure 3-1) became one of the most enduring images of the Confederacy, reproduced in widely circulated prints and evoked in a double equestrian statue dedicated in Baltimore in 1948. Lee's experience of loss and defeat would be as important to his image after the war as the prospect of victory had been to his fame during the war.

That defeat did not necessarily bring blame to Lee. Some commentators—including his most trusted subordinate commander, James Longstreet, and his final antagonist, U. S. Grant—held that Lee shared significant responsibility for the Confederate failure, but that opinion was decidedly a minority view for a century after the war. Army of Northern Virginia general Jubal Early and several of Lee's former staff officers played the most prominent roles in forging a consensus that Lee was a military genius with no American peer and that his forces "had been gradually worn down by the combined agencies

Figure 3-1. Frederick Halpin, after Everett B. D. Julio, *The Last Meeting of Lee and Jackson*, **1872 engraving of 1869 painting.** What sort of relationship between Lee and Jackson does this image describe?

The Museum of the Confederacy, Richmond, Virginia. Photography by Katherine Wetzel.

of numbers, steam-power, railroads, mechanism, and all the resources of physical science."[2] Their analysis, elaborated in many books and speeches and in the publications of the Richmond-based Southern Historical Society, blamed Confederate performance in the western theater and Lee's subordinates in Virginia for the southern failure to prevail before the northern advantages became overwhelming. They directed steady fire at the Gettysburg operations of Longstreet, who had the temerity both to criticize Lee for that Confederate disaster and to join the Republican party after the war. But if southern politics, self-interest in reputation, and personal loyalty to Lee may have influenced the viewpoint of the Southern Historical Society, other commentators reached similar conclusions. British writers contributed particularly significantly to Lee's reputation in the United States. Former British prime minister Winston Churchill summarized the overwhelming verdict almost a century after Appomattox when he declared Lee "one of the greatest captains known to the annals of war."[3]

A wider variety of opinion arose over the character traits that Lee had manifested in demonstrating such exemplary leadership. In an 1872 address, Jubal Early pinpointed the quality that would eventually become the central focus for debate over Lee's military record by repeatedly praising the "boldness, not to say audacity" of his attacks.[4] Early noted that "timid minds might regard this as rashness," but a popular anecdote linked Lee's charisma to his tendency to seize the initiative. Confederate authors John Thompson and Margaret Preston both wrote poems about a juncture in the battle of the Wilderness at which Lee took personal command of a wing of his army and prepared to lead an attack until Confederate soldiers chanting "Lee to the rear!" saw their commander led back into a safe position before they charged. Often recounted in war lore and illustrated in prints, the incident was one of many occasions on which Lee fulfilled the expectation that generals would share the burdens and dangers of the war.

Recognition of Lee as a singularly daring and aggressive commander created some tension with his reputation for extraordinary self-control. Confederate veteran and author John Esten Cooke wrote that no feature of Lee's personality was more striking than his "habit of preserving his calmness and equanimity under all circumstances." Cooke traced Lee's wartime success not to his boldness but to his level-headed judgment and capacity for "regular, deliberate, systematic work."[5] White southern admiration for Lee was virtually unanimous, but that agreement rested on different sets of values with potentially conflicting implications for the future of the region.

11

ABRAM JOSEPH RYAN

The Sword of Robert E. Lee

1867

Jubal Early once complained that "the domestic virtues, the moral worth, the unselfish patriotism and Christian purity of General Lee's character" were more widely understood than his merits as a commander.[6] This poem by Abram J. Ryan (see p. 39) was the most popular attempt to combine the two themes. What does Ryan indicate were the keys to Lee's prowess? Why does the poem, like other southern tributes, describe Lee and the Confederacy in terms reminiscent of a medieval legend?

> Forth from its scabbard, pure and bright,
>   Flashed the sword of Lee!
> Far in the front of the deadly fight,
> High o'er the brave in the cause of Right,
> Its stainless sheen, like a beacon light,
>   Led us to Victory!
>
> Out of its scabbard, where, full long,
>   It slumbered peacefully,
> Roused from its rest by the battle's song,
> Shielding the feeble, smiting the strong,
> Guarding the right, avenging the wrong,
>   Gleamed the sword of Lee!
>
> Forth from its scabbard, high in air
>   Beneath Virginia's sky—

Abram J. Ryan, *Poems: Patriotic, Religious, Miscellaneous*, 27th ed. (New York: P. J. Kennedy and Sons, 1908), 24–25.

And they who saw it gleaming there,
And knew who bore it, knelt to swear
That where that sword led they would dare
    To follow—and to die!

Out of its scabbard! Never hand
    Waved sword from stain as free,
Nor purer sword led braver band,
Nor braver bled for a brighter land,
Nor brighter land had a cause so grand,
    Nor cause a chief like Lee!

Forth from its scabbard! How we prayed
    That sword might victor be;
And when our triumph was delayed,
And many a heart grew sore afraid,
We still hoped on while gleamed the blade
    Of noble Robert Lee!

Forth from its scabbard all in vain
    Bright flashed the sword of Lee;
'Tis shrouded now in its sheath again,
It sleeps the sleep of our noble slain,
Defeated, yet without a stain,
    Proudly and peacefully!

A CROSSROADS ON MONUMENT AVENUE

As was often the case in nineteenth-century commemoration, planning for the disposition of Lee's body after his death in 1870 revealed different ideas about the best way to represent his legacy. Mary Randolph Custis Lee announced that she would bury her husband at the school he had led, renamed Washington & Lee College soon after his death. The decision stirred considerable controversy. A group of Richmond socialites formed the Ladies' Lee Monument Association in an effort to feature Lee's grave, adorned by a bronze equestrian statue, in the landscape of Confederate memory developing at Hollywood cemetery. Jubal Early led a parallel association of veterans, the Lee Monument Association, that also sought reinterment in the capital Lee had defended, where more former soldiers could visit the shrine than in remote Lexington. Standing by her decision, Lee's widow may have expected that Lexington would not remain remote, as Washington & Lee officers hoped the monument would help the school accelerate under new president Custis Lee the growth it had already enjoyed through its identification with his father.

While the Lee Memorial in Lexington moved toward completion, efforts continued to raise funds for an equestrian monument in Richmond. The separate campaigns appealed to different constituencies and sought to give different meanings to the monument. Early exhorted Lee's former army to "proclaim to all the ages, that the soldiers who fought under him remained true to him in death."[7] The Ladies' Lee Monument Association cast a much wider net, including a circular appeal sent to all churches in the South, and raised far more money than Early's organization. Virginia governor James L. Kemper, who had been wounded in Pickett's charge at Gettysburg, launched a new Lee monument campaign after white Democrats reclaimed the executive branch from an interracial Republican-Readjuster coalition, a "redemption" of the state that Kemper celebrated on October 26, 1875, by heading the first large-scale reunion of Confederate veterans at the dedication of a statue of Stonewall Jackson on the capitol grounds. Early turned the Lee Monument Association funds over to Kemper, but the clashing political styles of the two men caused tensions. One divisive issue was the proper expression of white dominance. An unabashedly belligerent racist, Early was appalled by Kemper's efforts to present an appearance of racial harmony by permitting African American militia to march at the rear of the Jackson parade. (The African American soldiers chose not to join the procession.) Early also despised the New South boosterism of Kemper, whose fundraising efforts for the Lee monument turned first to the urban bourgeoisie of the New South, whom he sought to reach through a circular sent to the mayors of southern cities.

The relationship between the Richmond remembrance of Lee and the ethos of enterprise in the New South became the focus for the most famous controversy over the location of a Civil War monument. Kemper's reinvigorated Lee Monument Association envisioned placement of the equestrian statue on the grounds of the state house, the site of all previous city monuments, while the Ladies' Lee Monument

Association looked toward the capitol, Hollywood cemetery, or a park overlooking the city. But Lee's nephew and former cavalry commander, Fitzhugh Lee, merging the two organizations as he led a new Democratic "redemption" of the state after the Republican-Readjuster coalition regained the governorship from 1879 to 1883, spearheaded adoption of a different plan. The governor's friend Otway S. Allen offered as a site for the monument eleven acres of an undeveloped fifty-eight-acre tract adjacent to the current city limits. The land around the monument was to be developed into a neighborhood centered on a boulevard that would extend the most exclusive residential street in Richmond and align the Lee Monument with the equestrian statue of Washington on the statehouse grounds.

The plan to use the Lee Monument as a fulcrum for real estate speculation drew varied reactions. Critics pointed out the irony in this self-representation of a region that often prided itself as the antithesis of Yankee commercialism. The governor nevertheless rallied sufficient support for "a plain business proposition" that expressed the prosperity and forward-looking enterprise of Richmond, which had recovered rapidly from the economic devastation of the war through the resurgence of iron production and flour milling and the emergence of tobacco processing. The Allen plan proved to be a financial success, and the central Monument Avenue became a showcase of Confederate memory as the Lee Monument was joined by monuments to Jefferson Davis (1907), J. E. B. Stuart (1907), Stonewall Jackson (1919), and Matthew Fontaine Maury (1929).

The design of the Lee Monument also sparked debate. Kemper's group held a design competition judged by a panel of veterans and politicians in 1877, and the Ladies' Lee Monument Association held a competition judged by leading artists in 1886. In the first competition, expatriate Virginia sculptor Moses Ezekiel presented a model of the general reining his horse Traveller in the heat of battle, atop a pedestal ornamented by an allegorical figure of Virginia mourning her dead (Figure 3-2). No models or pictures have survived of the composition that won this competition, submitted by the politically adroit sculptor Vinnie Ream Hoxie. Charles Niehaus's prize-winning entry in the second competition depicted a classically bareheaded Lee pacing a powerful charger. The merged associations did not award the commission to the young Niehaus, however, perhaps in response to the

Figure 3-2.   Moses Ezekiel, *Model for Proposed Monument to Lee,* **ca. 1877.**   What qualities of leadership does this composition identify in Lee?

Jacob Rader Marcus Center of the American Jewish Archives.

ridicule the model received for placing Lee on a bobtailed horse. One newspaper complained that the effeminate image was tantamount to representing Lee with "his hair banged."[8]

Instead the sponsors, evidently guided by lead juror Augustus Saint-Gaudens, awarded the commission to the famous French sculptor Antonin Mercié. Virginians had been appalled by Mercié's competition entry, which depicted Lee "as he passed among his dying troops on the field of Gettysburg—the horse rearing, the dying stretching for a last affectionate glance of their leader." Taking cues from Saint-Gaudens and the association, Mercié switched to an entirely different design (Figure 3-3). Viewers generally applauded the sculpture and the elaborate pedestal designed by French architect Paul Pujol, but Mercié maintained that his first model "would have been the most original if not the sublimest statue in the world."[9]

Art historian Kirk Savage has suggested that the sponsors preferred the calm and stability of the final design to Mercié's earlier proposal or Ezekiel's composition because the Lee equestrian monument served as a metaphor for the ostensibly harmonious system of racial repression envisioned by white southerners. As the white South had abandoned slavery, but not the determination to master blacks, "Lee's mastership had to be displaced, or represented by very subtle means." The Lee Monument provided a vehicle "in the relationship of the hero to his animal servant, the horse Traveller." Savage observes:

> The image of Lee on his horse worked beautifully as a model of leadership for a white supremacist society trying to legitimate its own authority.... The equestrian Lee is at once a retrospective image of the benevolent master, good to his inferiors, and a prospective image of a postwar white government claiming to know what is best for its own black population. The great power of this equestrian image was that it could bridge the old regime of slavery and the new regime of white rule without explicitly representing either; it helped legitimate the continuity between the two even as it disguised the physical and institutional forces that propped up both of them.[10]

At least one anecdote published in a Richmond newspaper treated mastery of Traveller as a test of racial hierarchy. Supposedly, when Virginia sculptor Edward Valentine asked to see the horse in action, Traveller "positively refused" to permit a "negro boy" to mount but accepted the authority of a Washington & Lee student. As Savage

Figure 3-3.   **Antonin Mercié and Paul Pujol,** *Unveiling of Lee Monument,* **Richmond, 1890.** What accounts for the differences between the design that Mercié preferred for the Lee Monument and the design that the sponsors accepted?

Valentine Richmond History Center.

notes, the story ignored the social reality that African Americans routinely exercised the horses of privileged white southerners. The Lee Monument, he reasons, similarly offered an image of white supremacism.[11]

This reading raises important questions about the interpretation of public monuments. If the equestrian Lee offers modern observers a striking metaphor for racial hierarchy in the postwar South, the historian must wonder whether contemporaries saw the same image. Certainly not all Virginians committed to white paternalism agreed that racial ideology should be the subject of the Lee Monument. Confederate veteran Moses Ezekiel, who explicitly incorporated white paternalism into his Confederate monument at Arlington Cemetery (Figure 2-2), proposed a straining, embattled Lee for the Richmond monument. The *Richmond Dispatch* offered an account of Mercié's work that associated the pose with Lee's command of white soldiers rather than black slaves.

> The sculptor represents General Lee as having just ridden to some eminence where he may better view the movements of the enemy, and here his soldiers recognizing his presence, greet him with one of those outbursts of cheers which never failed to welcome his presence among them, and as the General for a moment reins in his horse and acknowledges the greeting (by taking off his hat which he clutches in his right hand) the artist seizes the occasion to picture him.[12]

This narrative interpretation, related to the ideas about leadership explored by Ezekiel and by Mercié's first proposal, does not necessarily preclude the possibility that white southerners simultaneously saw the design of the monument as a metaphor for racial paternalism. Because the record of viewers' responses is limited, inferences must draw on the popular ideas about Lee that shaped perceptions of the monument.

The installation and dedication of the Lee Monument presented elaborate civic pageants in which race relations were one important motif. The few African American members of the Richmond City Council, which would become an all-white body after disfranchisement and redistricting in the early twentieth century, cast the only votes against the appropriation of funds for the cornerstone-laying ceremonies in 1886 and the dedication ceremonies on May 29, 1890. Councilmember and *Richmond Planet* editor John Mitchell reported that those who remembered the "clinking chains of slavery" would "keep silent" during the festivities.[13] Both ceremonies emphasized Lee's connection to Washington. James Barron Hope, who had anticipated secession in strident verses at the dedication of the equestrian Washington statue in 1858, declared in a poem for the Lee Monument cornerstone-laying:

Who shall blame the social order
Which gave us men as great as these?
Who condemn the soil of the forest
Which brings forth gigantic trees?
Who presume to doubt that Providence
Shapes out our destinies?[14]

Reenacting the 1858 hauling of the Washington statue from the James River to the state house, a crowd estimated at between 10,000 and 20,000 pulled the Lee Monument from the river to its place in 1890. White Richmonders treasured souvenir pieces of the ropes.

The Lee Monument dedication brought to peak level the popular participation in such ceremonies. Estimates of the size of the crowd at the dedication ranged up to 150,000; the parade stretched for four miles and included more than 15,000 Confederate veterans. The Civil War monument had clearly become an important theater of American memory.

12

JOHN W. DANIEL

Oration at the Dedication of the Lee Memorial in Lexington

June 28, 1883

A veteran of Lee's army, Daniel (1842–1910) was a leading opponent of the Readjuster coalition that he considered the vanguard of a state government controlled by Republicans, including African Americans. He was deeply involved in attempts to strengthen the Conservative faction (soon to be renamed the Democratic party) when he accepted the invitation to speak at the dedication of Lee's tomb at Washington & Lee College. One year after this speech he was elected to Congress, and in 1885 he moved to the Senate, where he remained until his

From *Ceremonies Connected with the Inauguration of the Mausoleum and the Unveiling of the Recumbent Figure of General Robert Edward Lee* (Lynchburg, Va.: J. P. Bell & Co., Printers, 1883), 26–82.

death. How does this speech illustrate the political potential in commemoration of Lee?

There was no happier or lovelier home than that of Colonel Robert Edward Lee, in the spring of 1861, when for the first time its threshold was darkened with the omens of civil war.

Crowning the green slopes of the Virginia Hills that overlook the Potomac, and embowered in stately trees, stood the venerable mansion of Arlington, facing a prospect of varied and imposing beauty. Its broad porch, and wide-spread wings, held out open arms, as it were, to welcome the coming guest. Its simple Doric columns graced domestic comfort with a classic air. Its halls and chambers were adorned with the portraits of patriots and heroes, and with illustrations and relics of the great revolution, and of the Father of his country. And within and without, history and tradition seemed to breathe their legends upon a canvass as soft as a dream of peace. . . .

So situated was Colonel Lee in the spring of 1861, upon the verge of the momentous revolution, of which he became so mighty a pillar and so glorious a chieftain. But we cannot estimate the struggle it cost him to take up arms against the Union—nor the sacrifice he made, nor the pure devotion with which he consecrated his sword to his native State—without looking beyond his physical surroundings, and following further the suggestions of his history and character, for the springs of action which prompted his course. Colonel Lee was emphatically a Union man; and Virginia, to the crisis of dissolution, was a Union state. He loved the Union with a soldier's ardent loyalty to the Government he served, and with a patriot's faith and hope in the institutions of his country. . . .

Unlike the statesmen of the hostile sections, who were constantly thrown into the provoking conflicts of political debate, he had been withdrawn by his military occupations from scenes calculated to irritate or chill his kindly feelings toward the people of the North; and on the contrary—in camp, and field, and social circle—he had formed many ties of friendship with its most esteemed soldiers and citizens. With the reticence becoming his military office, he had taken no part in the controversies which preceded the fatal rupture between the States—other than the good man's part, to "speak the soft answer that turns away wrath," and to plead for that forbearance and patience which alone might bring about a peaceful solution of the questions at issue. . . .

Where now is Robert Lee? On the border line, between two hostile empires, girding their loins for as stern a fight as ever tested warriors' steel, he beholds each beckoning to him to lead its people to battle. On the one hand, Virginia, now in the fore-front of a scarcely organized revolution, summons him to share her lot in the perilous adventure. The young Confederacy is without an army. There is no navy. There is no currency. There are few teeming work-shops and arsenals. There is little but a meagre and widely scattered population, for the most part men of the field, the prairie, the forest and the mountain, ready to stand the hazard of an audacious endeavor, to meet aggression with whatever weapons freemen can lay their hands on, and to carry high the banners of the free, whatever may betide.

Did he fail? Ah, did he fail? His beloved State would be trampled in the mire of the ways; the Confederacy would be blotted from the family of nations,—home and country would survive only in memory and in name; his people would be captives, their very slaves their masters; and he,—if of himself he thought at all,—he, mayhap, might have seen in the dim perspective, the shadow of the dungeon or the scaffold.

On the other hand stands the foremost and most powerful Republic of the earth, rich in all that handiwork can fashion or that gold can buy. It is thickly populated. Its regular army, and its myriad volunteers, rush to do its bidding. Its navy rides the Western seas in undisputed sway. Its treasury teems with the sinews of war, and its arsenals with weapons. And the world is open to lend its cheer and aid and comfort. Its capital lies in sight of his chamber window, and its guns bear on the portals of his home. A messenger comes from its President and from General Scott, Commander-in-Chief of its army, to tender him supreme command of its forces. Did he accept it, and did he succeed, the conqueror's crown awaits him, and win or lose, he will remain the foremost man of a great established nation, with all honor and glory that riches and office and power and public applause can supply.

Since the Son of Man stood upon the Mount, and saw "all the kingdoms of the earth and the glory thereof" stretched before him, and turned away from them to the agony and bloody sweat of Gethsemane, and to the Cross of Calvary beyond, no follower of the meek and lowly Saviour can have undergone more trying ordeal, or met it with higher spirit of heroic sacrifice.

There was naught on earth that could swerve Robert E. Lee from the path where, to his clear comprehension, honor and duty lay. To the statesman, Mr. Francis Preston Blair, who brought him the tender of supreme command, he answered:

"Mr. Blair, I look upon secession as anarchy. If I owned the four millions of slaves in the South, I would sacrifice them all to the Union. But how can I draw my sword against Virginia?"

Draw his sword against Virginia? Perish the thought! Over all the voices that called him he heard the still small voice that ever whispers to the soul of the spot that gave it birth, and of her who gave it suck; and over every ambitious dream, there rose the face of the angel that guards the door of home. . . .

And when the lines of battle formed, Robert Lee took his place in the line beside his people, his kindred, his children, his home. Let his defence rest on this fact alone. Nature speaks it. Nothing can strengthen it. Nothing can weaken it. The historian may compile; the casuist may dissect; the statesman may expatiate; the advocate may plead; the jurist may expound; but, after all, there can be no stronger or tenderer tie than that which binds the faithful heart to kindred and to home. And on that tie—stretching from the cradle to the grave, spanning the heavens, and riveted through eternity to the throne of God on high, and underneath in the souls of good men and true—on that tie rests, stainless and immortal, the fame of Robert Lee. . . .

Had the paroled soldier of Appomattox carried to retirement the vexed spirit and hollow heart of a ruined gamester, nothing had remained to him but to drain the dregs of a disappointed career. But there went with him that "consciousness of duty faithfully performed," which consoles every rebuff of fortune, sweetens every sorrow, and tempers every calamity. . . .

Lee thoroughly understood and thoroughly accepted the situation. He realized fully that the war had settled, settled forever, the peculiar issues which had embroiled it; but he knew also that only time could dissipate its rankling passions and restore freedom; and hence it was he taught that "Silence and patience on the part of the South was the true course"—silence, because it was vain to speak when prejudice ran too high for our late enemies to listen—patience, because it was the duty of the hour to labor for recuperation and wait for reconciliation. And murmuring no vain sigh over the "might have been," which now could not be—conscious that our destinies were irrevocably bound up with those of the perpetual Union, he lifted high over the fallen standards of war the banner of the Prince of Peace, emblazoned with "Peace on Earth and Good Will toward Men." . . .

As little things make up the sum of life, so they reveal the inward nature of men and furnish keys to history. It is in the office, the street, the field, the workshop, and by the fireside, that men show what stuff they are made of, not less than in those eventful actions which write themselves in lightnings across the skies and mark the rise and fall of nations. Nay, more—the highest attributes of human nature are not disclosed in action, but in self-restraint and repose. . . .

In action there is the stimulus of excited physical faculties, and of the moving passions—but in the composure of the calm mind that quietly devotes itself to hard life-work—putting aside temptations—contemplating and rising superior to all surroundings of adversity, suffering, danger and death, man is revealed in his highest manifestation. Then, and then alone, he seems to have redeemed his fallen state, and to be recreated in God's image. At the bottom of all true heroism is unselfishness. Its crowning expression is sacrifice. The world is suspicious of vaunted heroes. They are so easily manufactured. So many feet are cut and trimmed to fit Cinderella's slippers that we hesitate long before we hail the Princess. But when the true Hero has come, and we know that here he is, in verity, Ah! how the hearts of men leap forth to greet him—how worshipfully we welcome God's noblest work—the strong, honest, fearless, upright man.

In Robert Lee was such a hero vouchsafed to us and to mankind, and whether we behold him declining command of the Federal army to fight the battles and share the miseries of his own people; proclaiming on the heights in front of Gettysburg that the fault of the disaster was his own; leading charges in the crisis of combat; walking under the yoke of conquest without a murmur of complaint; or refusing fortunes to come here and train the youth of his country in the path of duty—he is ever the same meek, grand, self-sacrificing spirit. Here he exhibited qualities not less worthy and heroic than those displayed on the broad and open theatre of conflict, when the eyes of nations watched his every action. Here in the calm repose of civil and domestic duties, and in the trying routine of incessant tasks, he lived a life as high as when, day by day, he marshalled and led his thin and wasting lines, and slept by night upon the field that was to be drenched again in blood upon the morrow. . . .

Here, indeed, Lee, no longer the Leader, became, as it were, the Priest of his people, and the young men of Washington College were but a fragment of those who found in his voice and his example the shining signs that never misguided their footsteps. . . .

13

Newspaper Commentary
on the Lee Monument in Richmond

May 30–June 7, 1890

No Civil War monument dedication of the nineteenth century drew more national press coverage than the Richmond ceremonies for Lee. Many northern Republican newspapers deplored the commemoration of a traitor and applauded the decision by the 7th New York Regiment not to appear and the Secretary of War's refusal to permit U.S. Marine bands to play at the ceremonies. But northern Democratic newspapers

The first five excerpts are from *Public Opinion* 9 (June 7, 1890): 189–92, which also reprints other press commentary. The sixth excerpt is from the *Richmond Planet*, June 7, 1890.

and some Republican sheets, often noting the American as well as Confederate banners in the air at Richmond, considered the tribute harmless and well deserved. White southerners celebrated the occasion, although sometimes in different ways, while the *Richmond Planet* suggests the reactions of African Americans. Which of these viewpoints were gaining adherents, and which were becoming less widely shared? Which do you find most insightful?

Minneapolis Tribune, May 30

As a man General Lee had amiable and noble qualities, and as a soldier he was brave and brilliant; but he lacked the stuff that the highest type of hero is made of. The Lee cult is much in vogue, even at the North, in these days; and Englishmen under the lead of General Wolseley* are never weary of glorifying Lee at the expense of Grant, Sherman, and the great Northern generals. It is the fashion to surround him with a sort of halo of moral grandeur, military genius, and knightly grace, as a man of finer and better mold than his famous antagonists. With this worship let us emphatically disclaim sympathy. He was a good soldier because the United States Government had carefully trained him and had given him experience and promotion in the Mexican war and in other services. He was solemnly sworn to the defense of the Government. At the time when his services were most needed he deserted his post and took up arms against his country in a cause which never had his real approval. He would have been great in the highest sense if loyalty and firmness had been added to his other excellent qualities; but because he failed in these qualities he prolonged the horrors of a wicked war, and deepened the distress of his unhappy State. If Lee had remained in the Union army, true to his trust, what laurels might he not have won, and what brilliant services to humanity and to the whole country might he not have rendered? He made a fatal mistake, and it is not lightly to be condoned.

New York Mail and Express, May 31

It was providential that the rebel demonstrations in honor of Robert E. Lee, the typical Virginian aristocrat by lineage, culture, surroundings, and character, preceded the honors paid to the man who began his life in a log hut and his career of struggle on the towpath of a canal.[†] Lee's

---

*Garnet Joseph Wolseley (1833–1913) was a prominent British military commander.
†The James A. Garfield Monument in Cleveland was dedicated on May 30, 1890.

last and most useful work was done when he was college president. A college presidency was one of the first of the successive positions that Garfield won by pure force of will, grit, and genius. Lee was the natural demigod of the slave-holding oligarchy that sought to destroy the Union in order to establish a confederacy of which slavery was the cornerstone and essential element. Lee was not a conspirator, like the oligarchy that compassed secession by fraud, violence, tricks, and all other manner of crimes. He was the decorous and ornamental figure-head and the agent and tool of the oligarchs, after their diabolical plots had been consummated and "the Southern heart" had been "fired" by the bombardment of Fort Sumter.

New York Times, **May 30**

It is rather a pity that there were no organized bodies of representatives of the North at the unveiling of the monument to General Lee. The presence of Southern troops at the funeral of General Grant was recognized as a tribute as honorable to the men who paid it as to the memory of the hero to whom it was paid. A quarter of a century after the close of the war ought to suffice to put all its figures in an historical perspective. Everybody now recognizes that Falkland and Hampden* were both patriots according to their lights. Everybody ought to recognize now that there is no danger that the "issue" will arise again, that the soldiers of the Confederacy may have been as conscientious as the soldiers of the Union. Lee was the first of these. While he was no doubt doing what he believed to be his duty in "going with his State," there is no question at all that his conduct throughout the war, and after it, was that of a brave and honorable man. His memory is, therefore, a possession of the American people, and the monument that recalls it is itself a National possession.

Charleston News and Courier, **May 30**

The imposing demonstration at Richmond was a fitting tribute from the people of the South to the memory of the illustrious and incomparable soldier who led them in war, and it was such a tribute as no mere soldier, however successful or eminent in the arena of war, could win from any people. It was not a military demonstration alone, or mainly. The officers and men who, having followed the great commander through

---

*Lucius Cary, 2nd Viscount of Falkland (1610–1643), sided with Charles I. John Hampden (1594–1643) led the Parliamentary opposition to the king in the English Civil War.

the years of glorious but unavailing conflict, assembled themselves together yesterday to testify again their admiration and love for his exalted character, were only a small part of the vast throng that filled the streets of Richmond. The whole people of the South were represented in the throng, and by the throng, and the celebration can only be rightly understood when it is regarded as the expression of the profound and universal veneration of that people for a man to whom they have given the first place in their hearts because he had approved himself throughout his life, in war and in peace, to be most worthy of their devotion. No other people in the world, perhaps, and certainly not the people with whom we so recently contended in war, can comprehend fully the sentiment with which the people of the South regard the memory and even the name of Robert Lee. It is a name to conjure within every Southern home. His memory is as dear almost to the heart of every true son and daughter of the South as is that of the nearest and dearest of their own blood who, like him, have crossed the silent river. His sword was their defence in time of danger, and his fame is their defence still, throughout the world, when their history, character, and motives as a people are assailed by his enemies and theirs. He was himself a son of the South, a product of its peculiar and proud civilization, and as such the South claims him for her own.

New Orleans Picayune, May 30

When the Southern people gathered around the tomb of Robert Lee they but rendered homage and affection to one of the noblest and grandest and truest of the Americans. In Europe, when criticism deals with Americans, their character, their motives, and their achievements, it ignores the narrow and unseemly sectional hates and political hostilities. Robert Lee has been classed as the greatest of American field marshals, and one of the few of the world's mighty captains that have been admitted to the dignity of being classed with Alexander, Hannibal, Cæsar, and Napoleon. He gives honor to the race to which he belongs; his name and fame, when prejudice is dead, will live to glorify the annals of the great Republic. . . . When the cowards and the jobbers and the self-seekers shall be dead and gone to deserved oblivion, the names of the mighty dead of the Nation will be written in the halls of the Nation's history, and there will be not one to ask or to care if they were of the North or of the South.

Richmond Planet, June 7

The Negro was in the Northern processions on Decoration Day and in the Southern ones, if only to carry buckets of ice-water. He put up the

Lee Monument, and should the time come, will be there to take it down. He's black and sometimes greasy, but who could do without the Negro. . . .

You may say what you will the Negro is here to stay. Nothing goes on without him. He was in the Revolutionary War, the War of 1812, the Mexican War, the War of the Rebellion, and will be in every one that will take place in this country. . . .

An old colored man after seeing the mammoth parade of the ex-Confederates on May 29th and gazing at the rebel flags, exclaimed "The Southern white folks is on top—the Southern white folks is on top!" Afer thinking a moment, a smile lit up his countenance as he chuckled with evident satisfaction, "But we's got the government! We's got the government!" Yes, our party has the cations,* the most people will allow them to keep.

NATIONAL HERO

The northern reservations about Lee expressed at the dedication of the Richmond monument faded amid the growing celebration of sectional reconciliation in the 1890s. Fitzhugh Lee's prominent role in the Spanish-American War, first as consul general in Havana and later as a major-general of volunteers, further linked the family name to a burst of intersectional patriotism. The Hall of Fame for Great Americans selected the Confederate chieftain as one of its twenty-nine original inductees in 1901. Tributes during the 1907 centennial of Lee's birth included a commemorative poem by Julia Ward Howe, author of "The Battle Hymn of the Republic," and a call by President Theodore Roosevelt for the establishment of a permanent memorial in Washington. Charles Francis Adams Jr., a member of the most prominent New England family in American history, delivered the principal centennial address at Washington and Lee College.

Lee's national stature peaked in the second quarter of the twentieth century. Congress established the Robert E. Lee Memorial at Arlington in 1925 and funded restoration of the mansion to appear as it had when Lee last lived in it. Four years later a private association pur-

---

*Cations are positively charged ions that characteristically move toward the negatively charged cathode in electrolysis.

Figure 3-4.   Alexander Phimister Proctor, *Lee Memorial,* **Dallas, 1936.**   How did the adoption of Lee as a role model affect white southern culture?

From the collections of the Texas/Dallas History and Archives Division, Dallas Public Library.

chased Lee's birthplace, Stratford Hall, and launched a successful national fund-raising drive to restore that mansion. Adulatory writings about Lee climaxed with the wide readership and acclaim enjoyed by Douglas Southall Freeman's four-volume biography *R. E. Lee* (1934–1935) and his three-volume *Lee's Lieutenants: A Study in Command* (1942–1944), which together presented a lavishly detailed portrait of Lee as an almost flawless soldier and Virginia gentleman.

A group of socially prominent Dallas citizens more concisely expressed their admiration by commissioning an equestrian statue of the general with a young soldier who represented not the Confederate army but all southern youth who had looked to Lee for guidance during and since the war (Figure 3-4). Sculptor Alexander Phimister Proctor originally proposed to depict Lee "fighting a fierce struggle against fate and insurmountable odds," caught in a storm that pressed against his hat, his clothes, and his horse. But when the sponsors called for a more triumphant image, Proctor found that "the more I reviewed his character and his campaigns, the more I accepted the southern view that Lee himself had not been defeated," and he offered a different design.[15] President Franklin D. Roosevelt attended the 1936 dedication in Dallas, at which Reconstruction Finance Corporation chief Jesse Jones described Lee in the principal address as a paragon of the character traits that would sustain America during the Great Depression.

The celebration of Lee as a national hero created some tensions with alternative southern remembrance of the Confederacy. A particularly elaborate negotiation of memory developed after the 1914 launch of a campaign to carve a colossal statue of Lee onto the face of Stone Mountain, near Atlanta, which sculptor Gutzon Borglum soon shifted to a plan to depict Lee, Jackson, and Davis reviewing a procession of Confederate troops. Thirty-five-year-old William Simmons, an organizer and insurance salesman for a fraternal society, linked this initiative to the local excitement over director D. W. Griffiths's enormously influential film *Birth of a Nation* (1915), in which the rise of the Ku Klux Klan enabled ex-Confederates to regain control of the South and effect a sectional reconciliation cemented by white supremacism. On Thanksgiving night in 1915, Simmons led sixteen men, including the owner of Stone Mountain, to the crest of the monolith to reestablish the Ku Klux Klan by the light of a burning cross. Stone Mountain thereby became sacred ground to the Klan at the same time that Borglum's project benefited from the national veneration of Lee. (The bulk of its revenues came from the sale of commemorative Lee-Jackson coins minted by the U.S. Treasury in 1925.) This conjunction was in some ways not an obstacle to completion of the Stone Mountain project, for the second Klan was an intersectional organization in the mid-1920s, counting among its active members the Idaho-born Borglum. But the growing Klan emphasis on support for the Democratic party—the political bulwark of white supremacism in the South—led to conflicts with staunch northern Republicans like Borglum. The proposed Confederate memorial stalled after the firing of Borglum, and only when the state took over Stone Mountain in 1958 did carvings of Lee, Jackson, and Davis begin to advance steadily toward completion. Borglum, meanwhile, moved on to a similar project at Mount Rushmore.

Lee's national reputation similarly posed a problem for white southern writers who sought during the 1920s and 1930s to draw on regional history to criticize the materialism and spiritual emptiness of modern American life. The poet Donald Davidson made the most important attempt to incorporate Lee's image into this Southern Renascence. Davidson argued that American collective identity was "too abstract for a hero to thrive in it" and that "the Federal sphere will accommodate the statesman, but not the hero, in the epical and tremendous sense. . . . The sections, and within them the localities, are the true mothers of heroes." He complained that national commemoration tended to "surrender Lee the soldier and adhere only to the milder, more yielding Lee, the college president and quietist."[16] In his poem "Lee in the Mountains" (1934), Davidson portrayed Lee in restless retirement at Washington College, haunted by his wartime suggestion that the Confederate army might avoid defeat by taking refuge in the mountains. The work replied directly to the main oration delivered at the dedication of the Lee Monument in Richmond by Archer Anderson of the Tredegar Iron Works, the manufacturing stronghold of the Confederacy, in which Anderson had praised Lee's decision not to act on his mountain strategy as an astute recognition that modern war required the commander to remain in Richmond and defend his industrial base.

For the most part, Davidson's contemporaries focused not on Lee but on figures perceived as more distinctively southern. Allen Tate wrote biographies of Stonewall Jackson and Jefferson Davis. Particularly striking was the surge of interest in Nathan Bedford Forrest, the slavedealer-turned-cavalry-commander remembered most often in the immediate aftermath of the war for the massacre of surrendering black troops at Fort Pillow and his position as first Grand Wizard of the Ku Klux Klan. Forrest's shadow flickered across William Faulkner's novels about the complex southern legacy, and Andrew Nelson Lytle's *Bedford Forrest and His Critter Company* (1931) celebrated him as a champion of rural white southerners threatened by the industrial North.

If the national praise for Lee that remained strong through the Civil War centennial partly undercut his authority as a Confederate icon, his national stature in turn came under attack in the late twentieth century. Increased recognition of African Americans' rights to share in the shaping of the public sphere and changing white racial attitudes prompted critics to identify the Confederate commander more often with the Confederate commitment to slavery. Proposals to place statues of civil rights leaders on Monument Avenue—underscoring the racial content of the Confederate showcase and broadening the civic pantheon—ripened into action upon the death of Richmond native Arthur Ashe, a tennis star who had helped to break color barriers in that sport and had criticized racism in the United States and South Africa in addition to championing support for his fellow victims of the AIDS virus. After extensive and often heated debate, in July 1996 the city added to Monument Avenue a statue of Ashe holding a tennis racket and several books before a circle of admiring children. Three years later, controversy arose over the use of mural-sized photographs of prominent figures in Virginia history, including Lee in his Confederate uniform, to decorate a restored Richmond canal. The Richmond Historic Riverfront Foundation temporarily removed Lee's image before deciding to replace it with a postwar photograph. The decision acknowledged that many citizens continued to regard Lee as an important historical figure who did not warrant civic repudiation, but his positions on race and slavery had clearly become a liability to his reputation rather than an asset.

While defenders responded to the reassessment of Lee's politics and to the questioning of his military aggressiveness that became more common after the 1950s, it is not clear that Lee continued to inspire much popular enthusiasm by the end of the twentieth century. Only occasionally did the most dynamic forces in American culture renew his place in memory, as the Canadian-born musician Robbie Robertson did in his ballad "The Night They Drove Old Dixie Down" (1969), which invoked Lee's name as the personification of the fleeting transcendent in the hardscrabble life of a Confederate veteran. Other recent treatments of Lee have found him less heroic. Michael Shaara's *The Killer Angels* (1974), the most influential Civil War novel of the late twentieth century and the basis for the film *Gettysburg* (1993), presented Lee as an aging fatalist willing to gamble his men's lives on an all-or-nothing charge despite the protests of his far-seeing subordinate James Longstreet that the technology of modern warfare required patience and discipline rather than the providence and southern fighting spirit on which Lee relied. Jeff Shaara's novel *Gods and Generals*

(1996), a "prequel" to his father's work that was in turn adapted as a movie of the same title (2003), chose Stonewall Jackson rather than Lee as the central figure in its sympathetic treatment of the Confederate successes through the battle of Chancellorsville. Similarly, in his much-discussed commentary in Ken Burns's documentary television series *The Civil War* (1990), novelist Shelby Foote pointed to Nathan Bedford Forrest as the most exciting representative of the Confederacy. Forrest and Lincoln, he declared, were "the two absolute geniuses to emerge during the Civil War." A journalist visiting gatherings of Confederate enthusiasts in the late 1990s reported that shirts emblazoned with Forrest's picture outsold shirts featuring Lee fivefold.[17]

Revered by white southerners and widely admired by white northerners at the outset of the twentieth century, Lee held an uncertain position a century later. The shift was one of the most striking developments in the long sweep of Confederate commemoration, and it offered a promising clue into the changing meaning of Civil War remembrance.

14

CHARLES FRANCIS ADAMS JR.

Shall Cromwell Have a Statue?

1902

Great-grandson and grandson of presidents and son of the American minister to England during the war, Adams (1835–1915) served in cavalry units that often faced Lee's army. After the war he was a leading figure in the development of railroad regulation and president of the Union Pacific Railroad from 1884 to 1890. He also wrote extensively on American history. The Boer War prompted him to argue in "Lee at Appomattox" (1901) that Lee's decision not to try guerrilla tactics in

Charles Francis Adams, "Shall Cromwell Have a Statue?" in *Lee at Appomattox and Other Papers,* 2nd edition (Boston and New York: Houghton Mifflin and Company, 1902), 376–429.

1865 was a momentous and admirable recognition "that the United States, whether Confederate or Union, was a Christian community, and that his duty was to accept the responsibility which the fate of war had imposed upon him." Adams reprised this theme in "Shall Cromwell Have a Statue?" but he focused on Lee's decision to side with the Confederacy, which Adams framed with a highly romanticized description of Virginia slavery. What explanations does Adams's analysis suggest for the rise of northern admiration of Lee?

More than once already, on occasions not unlike this, have I quoted Oliver Wendell Holmes's remark in answer to the query of an anxious mother as to when a child's education ought to begin,—"About 250 years before it is born;" and it is a fact—somewhat necessitarian, doubtless, but still a fact—that every man's life is largely moulded for him far back in the ages. We philosophize freely over fate and free will, and one of the excellent commonplaces of our educational system is to instil into the minds of the children in our common schools the idea that every man is the architect of his own life. An admirable theory to teach; but, happily for the race, true only to a very limited extent. Heredity is a tremendous limiting fact. Native force of character—individuality— doubtless has something to do with results; but circumstances, ancestry, environment have much more. One man possibly in a hundred has in him the inherent force to make his conditions largely for himself; but even he moves influenced at every step from cradle to grave by antenatal and birth conditions. Take any man you please,—yourself, for instance; now and again the changes of life give opportunity, and the individual is equal to the occasion,—the roads forking, consciously or instinctively he makes his choice. Under such circumstances, he usually supposes that he does so as a free agent. The world so assumes, holding him responsible. He is nothing of the sort; or at best such only in a very limited degree. . . .

Of [Lee] it might, and in justice must, be said, that he was more than of the essence, he was of the very quintessence of Virginia. In his case, the roots and fibres struck down and spread wide in the soil, making him of it a part. A son of the revolutionary "Light-Horse Harry," he had married a Custis.* His children represented all there was of descent, blood, and tradition of the Old Dominion, made up as the Old Dominion was of tradition, blood, and descent. The holder of broad patrimonial acres, by birth and marriage he was a slave-owner, and a slave-owner of the patriarchal type, holding "slavery, as an institution, a moral and political evil." Every sentiment, every memory, every tie conceivable

---

*Lee's wife was Mary Randolph Custis, whose father had grown up at Mount Vernon as Washington's adopted son.

bound him to Virginia; and when the choice was forced upon him,—
had to be made,—sacrificing rank, career, the flag, he threw in his lot
with Virginia. . . .

[Lee's] lights may have been wrong,—according to our ideas then
and now they were wrong; but they were his lights, and, acting in full
accordance with them, he was right.

But, to those thus speaking, it is sometimes replied, "Even tolerance
may be carried too far, and is apt then to verge dangerously on what
may be better described as moral indifference. . . . This will not do.
Some moral test must be applied,—some standard of right and wrong.

"It is by the recognition and acceptance of these that men prominent
in history must be measured, and approved or condemned. To call it
our Civil War is but a mere euphemistic way of referring to what was in
fact a slaveholders' rebellion, conceived and put in action for no end but
to perpetuate and extend a system of human servitude, a system the
relic of barbarism, an insult to advancing humanity. To the furtherance
of this rebellion, Lee lent himself. Right is right, and treason is treason;
and as that which is morally wrong cannot be right, so treason cannot
be other than a crime. Why, then, because of sentiment, or sympathy,
or moral indifference, seek to confound the two? Charles Stuart and
Cromwell* could not both have been right. If Thomas[†] was right, Lee
was wrong."

To this I would reply, that we, who take another view, neither confound, nor seek to confound, right with wrong, or treason with loyalty.
We accept the verdict of time; but, in so doing, we insist that the verdict
shall be in accordance with the facts, and that each individual shall be
judged on his own merits, and not stand acquitted or condemned in
block. . . . In the second place, the passage of the centuries works won-
ders, especially in the views men hold of the causes and incidents of
civil strife. We get at last to see that the right is never wholly on one
side; that in the grand result all the elements were fused. Things then
are seen with other eyes. . . .

In all these matters, time is the great magician. It both mellows and
transforms. The Englishman of to-day does not apply to Cromwell the
standard of loyalty or treason, of right and wrong, applied after the
Restoration; nor again does the twentieth century confirm the nineteenth's verdicts. Even slavery we may come to regard as a phase, par-
donable as passing, in the evolution of a race.

I hold it will certainly be so with our Civil War. . . . True! The moral
right, the spirit of nationality, the sacred cause of humanity even, were

---

*Charles I and Oliver Cromwell represented the opposing sides in the English Civil
War that toppled the Stuart dynasty.

[†]General George H. Thomas, also a Virginia native, fought with distinction for the
Union.

on our side; but, among those opposed, and who in the end went down, were men not less sincere, not less devoted, not less truly patriotic according to their lights, than he who among us was first in all those qualities,—men of whom it was and is a cause of pride and confidence to say, "They, too, were countrymen!"

Typical of those men—most typical—was Lee. He represented, indi-vidualized, all that was highest and best in the Southern mind and the Confederate cause,—the loyalty to state, the keen sense of honor and personal obligation, the slightly archaic, the almost patriarchal, love of dependent, family, and home. As I have more than once said, he was a Virginian of the Virginians. He represents a type which is gone,— hardly less extinct than that of the great English nobleman of the feudal times, or the ideal head of the Scotch clan of a later period; but just so long as men admire courage, devotion, patriotism, the high sense of duty and personal honor,—all, in a word, which go to make up what we know as Character,—just so long will that type of man be held in affec-tionate, reverential memory. . . .

NOTES

[1] George Washington Cable, "The Silent South," *Century* 30 (September 1885): 674.

[2] Jubal A. Early, "The Campaigns of Gen. Robert E. Lee," in *Lee the Soldier,* edited by Gary W. Gallagher (Lincoln: University of Nebraska Press, 1996), 67.

[3] Winston Churchill, *A History of the English-Speaking Peoples,* 4 vols. (New York: Dodd, Mead, 1956–1958), 4:169.

[4] Early, "Campaigns of Lee," 42.

[5] John Esten Cooke, "The Personal Character of General Lee," *Appleton's Journal of Literature, Science, and Art* 13 (January 9, 1875): 48, 50.

[6] Early, "Campaigns of Lee," 38.

[7] Ibid., 73.

[8] Kirk Savage, *Standing Soldiers, Kneeling Slaves: Race, War, and Monument in Nineteenth-Century America* (Princeton, N.J.: Princeton University Press, 1997), 144.

[9] Richmond *Dispatch,* May 25, 1890.

[10] Savage, *Standing Soldiers,* 135.

[11] Ibid., 133–34.

[12] *Richmond Dispatch,* May 25, 1890. Archer Anderson offered a similar reading in his dedication address.

[13] Savage, *Standing Soldiers,* 152.

[14] *Richmond Dispatch,* May 29, 1890.

[15] Alexander Phimister Proctor, *Sculptor in Buckskin* (Norman: University of Okla-homa Press, 1971), 192.

[16] Donald Davidson, "A Note on American Heroes," *Southern Review* 1 (1935–1936): 436.

[17] Court Carney, "The Contested Image of Nathan Bedford Forrest," *Journal of Southern History* 67 (August 2001): 626, 628.

4

Representative Regiment:
The 54th Massachusetts

The 54th Massachusetts Volunteer Infantry Regiment has provided a focus for public remembrance of the racial issues that Civil War commemoration has often obscured. The first regiment of African American soldiers and white officers authorized to form in the free states, the 54th Massachusetts was from its inception a showcase for the shift in policy that would eventually bring about 180,000 African Americans into the Union ranks. Prominent African Americans across the North led the recruitment campaign for the regiment; Frederick Douglass's sons Lewis and Charles were among the men who enlisted. Massachusetts governor John A. Andrew added to the spotlight on the unit by selecting as its colonel Robert Gould Shaw, the twenty-five-year-old son of wealthy and well-connected Boston abolitionists who had recently moved to Staten Island. The departure of the regiment from Boston on May 28, 1863, before a large crowd stirred the excitement more common in such scenes at the beginning of the war. Former slave Harriet Jacobs later recalled that as she watched "my heart swelled with the thought that my poor oppressed race were to strike a blow for Freedom! Were at last to help in breaking the chains."[1]

The regiment's courage in leading the Union assault on Fort Wagner, a massive Confederate earthwork outside Charleston, South Carolina, on the night of July 18, 1863, dispelled any doubts about the valor of African American soldiers that remained after the strong performance at Port Hudson (May 27) and Milliken's Bend, Louisiana (June 7), of regiments comprised of "contrabands," or escaped slaves in Union service. Of the 600 members of the 54th Massachusetts who participated in the charge at Fort Wagner, 272 were killed, wounded, or captured in a fierce battle. Shaw was shot through the heart at the top of the parapet, which African American soldiers held briefly before retreating. When they regrouped, Sergeant William Carney carried the national colors although he had been shot twice; he reportedly told the comrades he met in a field hospital, "The dear old flag never touched the ground, boys." The next morning, Confederates stripped Shaw's body and dropped it in a ditch with the African American rank and file, while burying the other dead white officers separately. Northern sources reported that Confederate commander Johnson Hagood had snarled, "He is buried with his niggers."[2]

The timing of the charge on Fort Wagner helped to bring the 54th Massachusetts even wider notice than previous interest in the regiment and the drama of events on July 18 ensured. The assault took place on the day after federal troops ended the New York City draft riots, the most violent urban uprising that had yet taken place in the United States. Administration supporters contrasted the murderers and looters with Shaw, whose family narrowly escaped the Staten Island offshoot of the riots, and with the African Americans who had given their lives for their country only days after the seven-year-old nephew of Sergeant Robert J. Simmons was stoned to death in New York. The fame of the regiment became so intertwined with the expansion of African American enlistment that the *New York Tribune* could claim at the end of the war that "if this Massachusetts Fifty-fourth had faltered when its trial came, Two Hundred Thousand colored troops for whom it was a pioneer would never have been put into the field."[3]

EPITAPHS FOR AN UNMARKED GRAVE

Early commemoration of the 54th Massachusetts often concentrated on the burial of Shaw with the African American troops. Poems like "One Grave" and "A Monument to Colonel Shaw" declared that the Confederate expression of disdain for the commander had created the perfect memorial. The symbol of the shared grave received an additional burst of publicity when Shaw's father, observing that "a soldier's most appropriate burial-place is on the field where he has fallen," instructed the general commanding the Department of the South that he did not wish his son's body to be recovered by the advancing Union troops who took Fort Wagner in early September 1863.[4]

The theme of interracial unity notwithstanding, commemoration of the 54th Massachusetts was subject from the outset to tension between emphases on Shaw and on the African American rank and file. One strand of remembrance, most evident at Harvard University, stressed that Shaw had vindicated the leadership claims of the Boston social elite. Within days of the Fort Wagner assault, historian Francis Parkman wrote in a newspaper essay that "the necrology of Harvard" proved the vitality of a "Brahmin caste" that had "yielded a progeny of gentlemen and scholars from the days of the Puritans" and now promised to rescue the country from its "ultra-democratic fallacies."[5] In 1890, wealthy alumnus and Civil War veteran Henry Lee Higginson donated a large tract of land to Harvard for an athletic complex to be called Soldier's Field in honor of Shaw and five other young Brahmins who died in the war. At a speech on the occasion of the gift, Higginson told students to follow their Civil War predecessors in recognizing that "everywhere we see the signs of ferment—questions social, moral, physical, economical. The pot is boiling hard and you must tend it . . . helping, sympathizing, and so guiding and restraining others, who have less education, perhaps, than you."[6]

But memory of the 54th Massachusetts did not always focus on Shaw. Historian Alice Fahs has noted that after the assault on Fort Wagner "popular images of black soldiers began to shift dramatically toward a forthright celebration of black courage and especially black manhood." Louisa May Alcott's short story "The Brothers" (1863) and Rebecca Harding Davis's novel *Waiting for the Verdict* (1868) were among the literary works that featured fictional soldiers of the 54th Massachusetts. The protagonists died in both of these tales, as in the wartime poems honoring black valor at Fort Wagner, and Fahs points out that "northerners were only too willing to celebrate the manhood of black soldiers who no longer had any manhood to exercise."[7] But the 54th Massachusetts also provided an important model for a more radical development she identifies: the emerging image of African American soldiers not as martyrs but as citizens who would survive the war and reshape the republic. William Carney assumed a leading place in the cluster of wartime celebrities honored for acts of devotion to the national colors. He appeared alongside the dying Shaw in the charge at Morris Island as imagined by printmakers Currier and Ives (Figure 4-1) and later Kurz and Allison (1890). Edmonia Lewis, a

Figure 4-1. Currier and Ives, *The Gallant Charge of the Fifty-Fourth Massachusetts (Colored) Regiment*, 1863. What significance do you attach to the depiction of the black flagbearer in this print?

Library of Congress.

THE GALLANT CHARGE OF THE FIFTY FOURTH MASSACHUSETTS (COLORED) REGIMENT.

On the Rebel works at Fort Wagner, Morris Island near Charleston, July 18th 1863, and death of Colonel Robt G. Shaw.

sculptor of Ojibway and African American descent, exhibited a small statue of Carney kneeling to keep the flag above the ground. In 1868, Anna Dickinson based a character partly on Carney in a novel that advocated black suffrage, *What Answer?* Remembrance of Carney continued with such poems as George Clinton Rowe's "The Old Flag" (1890) and James M. Guthrie's "The Old Flag Never Touched the Ground" (1899), and it culminated in 1900 with the award of the Congressional Medal of Honor.

Although prints and poems and historical writings acknowledged the contributions of the 54th Massachusetts and other African American soldiers, George Washington Williams observed in his *History of Negro Troops in the Rebellion* (1887) that these initiatives could not take the place of recognition in a public space. The African American veteran and intellectual called on Congress to commission a monument at Howard University to the 36,847 African American soldiers who died in the Union army; the park surrounding the monument was to be named for Shaw. Legislation drafted by Williams passed the Senate but failed in the House of Representatives, and the idea remained dormant for a century.

15

ANNA QUINCY WATERSTON

Together

August 1863

The family names that Anna Cabot Lowell Quincy (1812–1899) brought into her marriage to Unitarian minister Robert Cassie Waterston placed her at the center of the most influential social circles in nineteenth-century Boston. This poem, published a few weeks after the assault on Fort Wagner, typifies local high society's response to that drama. How does Waterston differentiate between Shaw and the rank and file? Why does she describe the fallen soldiers, most of whom were born in nonslaveholding states, as "freedmen"?

[Sarah Shaw, comp.], *Memorial R.G.S.* (Cambridge, Mass.: University Press, 1864), 112.

O fair-haired Northern hero,
  With thy guard of dusky hue!
Up from the field of battle,
  Rise to the last review.

Sweep downward, holy angels,
  In legions dazzling bright,
And bear these souls together
  Before Christ's throne of light.

The Master, who remembers
  The cross, the thorns, the spear,
Smiles on the risen freedmen,
  As their ransomed souls appear.

And thou, young, generous spirit,
  What will thy welcome be?
"Thou hast aided the down-trodden,
Thou hast done it unto ME!"

16

FRANCES ELLEN WATKINS HARPER

The Massachusetts Fifty-Fourth

October 1863

Born free in Baltimore, Frances Ellen Watkins Harper (1825–1911) was one of the most popular African American poets and antislavery orators in the mid-nineteenth-century United States. She published "The Massachusetts Fifty-Fourth" in *Anglo-African,* the leading black newspaper in the country, about three months after the assault on Fort Wagner. After the Civil War she spoke extensively for equal rights for African Americans, women's suffrage, and temperance. She also reexamined the war in many writings, including her full-length novel about

New York *Anglo-African,* October 10, 1863.

race and slavery, *Iola Leroy, or Shadows Uplifted* (1892). How would you compare Harper's description of the 54th Massachusetts with Anna Quincy Waterston's poem?

Where storms of death were sweeping,
Wildly through the darkened sky,
Stood the bold but fated column,
Brave to do, to dare, and die.

With cheeks that knew no blanching,
And brows that would not pale;
Where the bloody rain fell thickest,
Mingled with the fiery hail.

Bearers of a high commission
To break each brother's chain;
With hearts aglow for freedom,
They bore the toil and pain.

And onward pressed though shot and shell
Swept fiercely round their path;
While batteries hissed with tongues of flame,
And bayonets flashed with wrath.

Oh! not in vain those heroes fell,
Amid those hours of fearful strife;
Each dying heart poured out a balm
To heal the wounded nation's life.

And from the soil drenched with their blood,
The fairest flowers of peace shall bloom;
And history cull rich laurels there,
To deck each martyr hero's tomb.

And ages yet uncrossed with life,
As sacred urns, do hold each mound
Where sleep the loyal, true, and brave
In freedom's consecrated ground.

BLACK AND WHITE IN BRONZE

Shortly after the charge on Fort Wagner, African American business-man and civic activist Joshua B. Smith suggested to Senator Charles Sumner that a monument commemorating the event should be placed in Boston. The two men launched the project a few months after the close of the war. As Smith explained, they desired a statue that would depict Shaw on horseback, as the city "last saw him at the head of his regiment on Beacon street."[8] Although Governor John A. Andrew chaired the monument committee, Sumner remained in control from the outset. This concentration of authority alienated some early sup-porters of the undertaking, and momentum stalled altogether as Sum-ner became immersed in Congressional debates over Reconstruction and Andrew emerged as a likely challenger for his Senate seat.

After the deaths of Andrew in 1867 and Sumner in 1874, and after a much-publicized centennial celebration of the battle of Lexington at which General Roswell Ripley of South Carolina returned the captured battle flag of the 54th Massachusetts, monument committee treasurer Edward Atkinson revived interest in the initiative. A politically active businessman, Atkinson formed a new committee that collected further contributions, still almost entirely from a small circle of elite Bostoni-ans. Social exclusivity also played a part in the commissioning of artists to design the monument, as Atkinson was a neighbor of renowned architect Henry Hobson Richardson in the fashionable sub-urb of Brookline. Richardson proposed to design a setting for a statue by Augustus Saint-Gaudens, with whom he had worked on his cele-brated Trinity Church in Boston. In April 1882 a Boston newspaper reported that the committee had approved a monument to be placed along the fence in front of the Massachusetts statehouse. The design featured a statue of Shaw mounted beneath an arch supported by columns; next to the columns would be panels depicting the departure of the volunteers from the city, the charge at Fort Wagner, and the return of the regiment to Boston (Figure 4-2).

The Shaw family objected to this adoption of the equestrian pro-gram suggested by Smith, which Sumner had endorsed as a demo-cratic appropriation of a sculptural form originally reserved to Roman emperors and later used as an emblem of European royalty. "As an American citizen [Shaw] belonged to our sovereignty," Sumner had

Figure 4-2.   Office of H. H. Richardson, *Drawing of Proposed Shaw Memorial,* **ca. 1882.**   How did placement of the Shaw Memorial at the Massachusetts statehouse reinforce its intended themes?

H. H. Richardson Papers, MON B1, Department of Printing and Graphic Arts, Houghton Library, Harvard College Library.

argued, "and we fitly celebrate him with the highest honors." But the Shaw family objected that an equestrian statue "seemed pretentious" for a soldier who was not of the highest rank.[9] By spring 1883, Saint-Gaudens had prepared a new design. Consistent with the original sponsors' desire to represent the departure from Boston, Saint-Gaudens proposed to depict Shaw on horseback in high relief with the regiment marching alongside him in much lower relief; a female figure floated overhead beneath an arched top. He signed a contract in February 1884 to produce the sculpture within two years for $15,000.

The work (Figure 4-3) instead took him thirteen years to finish, partly because the modest compensation made him feel justified in

Figure 4-3. Augustus Saint-Gaudens and Charles McKim, *Shaw Memorial,* **Boston, 1884–1897.** To what extent does this monument treat Shaw and African Americans as fellow citizens? Library of Congress.

devoting time to the more lucrative commissions that streamed into his studio and partly because of the changes he made in his plan. Saint-Gaudens's most important modification was to deepen the reliefs of the soldiers he had introduced to escape from an exclusive focus on Shaw. He later recalled that "the negroes assumed far more importance than I had originally intended."[10] These representations have attracted considerable comment. Saint-Gaudens chose not to base the reliefs on photographs of soldiers in the regiment, as he had done with the portrait of Shaw, but instead worked from the heads of African American men he recruited in New York and Boston. He sculpted about forty heads in clay as studies for the twenty-one recognizable African American faces on the monument. Critics of Saint-Gaudens have argued that he regarded the recruited models with a racism reflected in his depictions of the soldiers and also in an overall design that placed Shaw above the rank and file, reaching alone into the realm of the angel. Unquestionably, Saint-Gaudens's memoirs describe the African American models in belittling terms as simple-minded creatures noteworthy mostly as physical objects and for the amusement they brought to the studio. Saint-Gaudens's defenders have answered that his commitment to realism did not permit him to carry these prejudices into his work. They argue that the depictions of African Americans in the Shaw Memorial are remarkable precisely because they depart from racial stereotypes and present a variety of highly individuated, sensitively rendered African American faces.

Saint-Gaudens also devoted much time and effort to reworkings of the floating female figure. Some observers suggested that the ideal element weakened his highly realistic composition. Upon receiving a photograph of an early version, French sculptor Paul Bion told his friend, "Your negroes marching in step and your Colonel leading them told me enough. Your priestess merely bores me as she tries to impress upon me the beauty of their action."[11] Saint-Gaudens declined to eliminate the figure and sought to integrate the real and the ideal. Originally the figure faced outward at Shaw and carried palms and poppies. Saint-Gaudens turned the figure's head more to a profile and replaced the palms with an olive branch of peace that he thought "looks less 'Christian martyr-like.'"[12]

Saint-Gaudens's work invited comparison with other depictions of citizens leaving for war. His image of the soldiers challenged a literary

and visual convention in which volunteers' farewells to women constituted the defining feature of a departure scene (Figure 2-2). His rigor-
ous realism also contrasted sharply with a famous departure
monument that similarly took the form of a high relief: François
Rude's *Departure of the Volunteers in 1792* (Figure 4-4), an emblem of
France since its unveiling on the Arc de Triomphe in Paris in 1836.
Saint-Gaudens capped his effort to create an icon of the citizen-soldier
by inscribing on his panel the Latin motto of the Society of the Cincinnati: "Omnia relinquit servare rempublicam" ("He gave all to serve
the republic"). Like much commemoration of the 54th Massachusetts,
the quotation lent itself to a reading that stressed the privileges of
Shaw, whose ancestry entitled him to membership in the organization
of Revolutionary War officers and their descendants, or to an interpretation that recognized all members of the regiment as carrying
forward the example of Cincinnatus and the ideals of the Revolution.

As Saint-Gaudens slowly brought his work to completion, the monument committee conducted a long debate over the inscription and
then turned to planning the dedication ceremony, in which the most
important part was selection of the orators. Like most organizers of
such programs, they thought first of veterans. Atkinson, who would
emerge in the next year as a prominent critic of the Spanish-American
War, vetoed Oliver Wendell Holmes Jr. on the grounds that his "Soldier's Faith" address (Document 5) had been "brutal." After a refusal
from Colonel Thomas Livermore, the committee followed the recommendation of the Shaw family and chose Harvard professor William
James, with Booker T. Washington invited "for what might be considered a response on behalf of his race."[13] The selection of James led to
some difficulty, for although his brother Garth Wilkinson James had
participated in the assault on Fort Wagner as adjutant of the 54th
Massachusetts, William James had avoided wartime military service.
Henry Lee Higginson headed a delegation of veterans who asked that
the monument committee "have an 'old soldier' say something." The
resolution of this protest was an address by Higginson at Harvard
Memorial Hall on the day before the dedication, in which he criticized
"intemperate" abolitionists who had "despaired of their country's
virtue and wisdom" and saluted Shaw and his fellow soldiers who had
"atoned, so far as in them lay, for the sin of slavery."[14]

Figure 4-4. François Rude, *Departure of the Volunteers in 1792,* **Arc de Triomphe de l'Étoile, Paris, 1833–1836.** How does the Shaw Memorial respond to this influential sculpture?

The dedication on May 31, 1897, was, as William James told his novelist brother Henry, "an extraordinary occasion for sentiment." He reported that the weeping skies harmonized with the pathos of "the last wave of the war breaking over Boston, everything softened and made poetic and unreal by distance, poor little Robert Shaw erected into a great symbol of deeper things than he ever realized himself."[15] Booker T. Washington observed in his autobiography *Up from Slavery* (1901) that he had never seen a demonstration like the clamor that followed when he referred in his speech to William Carney and the sergeant rose from his seat, waving the American flag he had saved at Fort Wagner. Like James and Washington, Saint-Gaudens was deeply touched by the sight of the African American veterans who marched in procession along Beacon Street. "The impression of those old soldiers, passing the very spot where they left for the war so many years before, thrills me even as I write these words," he later recalled. "They faced and saluted the relief, with the music playing 'John Brown's Body,' a recall of what I had heard and seen thirty years before from my cameo-cutter's window. They seemed as if returning from the war, the troops of bronze marching in the opposite direction, the direction in which they had left for the front, and the young men there represented now showing these veterans in the vigor and hope of youth. It was a consecration."[16]

17

WILLIAM JAMES

Oration at Dedication of the Shaw Memorial
May 31, 1897

James (1842–1910) joined the Harvard faculty in 1872, working first in the field of psychology and later in philosophy. His comments on the development of human nature in this address reflect some of the ideas

From *The Monument to Robert Gould Shaw: Its Inception, Completion and Unveiling, 1865–1897* (Boston: Houghton Mifflin and Company, 1897), 73–87.

of his momentous *Principles of Psychology* (1890), including a concern with the ways in which social Darwinists had applied concepts of evolution. James's oration replied directly to the arguments that Oliver Wendell Holmes Jr., an intellectual sparring partner of his youth, had advanced two years earlier in "The Soldier's Faith" and marked an important step in James's emergence as a critic of American militarism and imperialism, which culminated in his famous essay "The Moral Equivalent of War" (1910). What did James find most admirable about Shaw? Do you agree with James that his speech was "as 'abolitionist' in tone as anyone can desire"?

The historic importance of an event is measured neither by its material magnitude, nor by its immediate success. Thermopylae was a defeat; but to the Greek imagination, Leonidas and his few Spartans stood for the whole worth of Grecian life. Bunker Hill was a defeat; but for our people, the fight over that breastwork has always seemed to show as well as any victory that our forefathers were men of a temper not to be finally overcome. And so here. The war for our Union, with all the constitutional questions which it settled, and all the military lessons which it gathered in, has throughout its dilatory length but one meaning in the eye of history. . . . And nowhere was that meaning better symbolized and embodied than in the constitution of this first Northern negro regiment.

Look at the monument and read the story—see the mingling of elements which the sculptor's genius has brought so vividly before the eye. There on foot go the dark outcasts, so true to nature that one can almost hear them breathing as they march. State after State by its laws had denied them to be human persons. The Southern leaders in congressional debates, insolent in their security, loved most to designate them by the contemptuous collective epithet of "this peculiar kind of property." There they march, warm-blooded champions of a better day for man. There on horseback, among them, in his very habit as he lived, sits the blue-eyed child of fortune, upon whose happy youth every divinity had smiled. Onward they move together, a single resolution kindled in their eyes, and animating their otherwise so different frames. The bronze that makes their memory eternal betrays the very soul and secret of those awful years. . . .

Our nation had been founded in what we may call our American religion, baptized and reared in the faith that a man requires no master to take care of him, and that common people can work out their salvation well enough together if left free to try. But the founders of the Union had not dared to touch the great intractable exception; and slavery had wrought and spread, until at last the only alternative for the nation was to fight or die. What Shaw and his comrades stand for and show us is that in such an emergency Americans of all complexions and conditions can go forth like brothers, and meet death cheerfully if need be, in order that this religion of our native land shall not become a failure on earth.

We of this Commonwealth believe in that religion; and it is not at all because Robert Shaw was an exceptional genius, but simply because he was faithful to it as we all may hope to be faithful in our measure when occasion serves, that we wish his beautiful image to stand here for all time, an inciter to similarly unselfish public deeds.

Shaw thought but little of himself, yet he had a personal charm which, as we look back on him, makes us say with the poet: "None knew thee but to love thee, none named thee but to praise." This grace of nature was united in him in the happiest way with a filial heart, a cheerful ready will, and a judgment that was true and fair. And when the war came, and great things were doing of the kind that he could help in, he went as a matter of course to the front. What country under heaven has not thousands of such youths to rejoice in, youths on whom the safety of the human race depends? Whether or not they leave memorials behind them, whether their names are writ in water or in marble, depends mostly on the opportunities which the accidents of history throw into their path. Shaw recognized the vital opportunity: he saw that the time had come when the colored people must put the country in their debt.

Colonel Lee has just told us something about the obstacles with which this idea had to contend. For a large party of us this was still exclusively a white man's war; and should colored troops be tried and not succeed, confusion would grow worse confounded. Shaw was a captain in the Massachusetts Second, when Governor Andrew invited him to take the lead in the experiment. He was very modest, and doubted, for a moment, his own capacity for so responsible a post. We may also imagine human motives whispering other doubts. Shaw loved the Second Regiment, illustrious already, and was sure of promotion where he stood. In this new negro-soldier venture, loneliness was certain, ridicule inevitable, failure possible; and Shaw was only twenty-five; and, although he had stood among the bullets at Cedar Mountain and Antietam, he had till then been walking socially on the sunny side of life. But whatever doubts may have beset him, they were over in a day, for he inclined naturally towards difficult resolves. He accepted the proffered command, and from that moment lived but for one object, to establish the honor of the Massachusetts 54th. . . .

Robert Shaw quickly inspired others with his own love of discipline. There was something almost pathetic in the earnestness with which both the officers and men of the 54th embraced their mission of showing that a black regiment could excel in every virtue known to man.

They had good success, and the 54th became a model in all possible respects. . . .

How soon, indeed, are human things forgotten! As we meet here this morning, the Southern sun is shining on their place of burial, and the waves sparkling and the sea-gulls circling around Fort Wagner's ancient site.* But the great earthworks and their thundering cannon, the commanders and their followers, the wild assault and repulse that for a brief space made night hideous on that far-off evening, have all sunk into the blue gulf of the past, and for the majority of this generation are hardly more than an abstract name, a picture, a tale that is told. Only when some yellow-bleached photograph of a soldier of the 'sixties comes into our hands, with that odd and vivid look of individuality due to the moment when it was taken, do we realize the concreteness of that bygone history, and feel how interminable to the actors in them were those leaden-footed hours and years. The photographs themselves erelong will fade utterly, and books of history and monuments like this alone will tell the tale. The great war for the Union will be like the siege of Troy, it will have taken its place amongst all other "old, unhappy, far-off things and battles long ago."

Ah, my friends, and may the like of it never be required of us again!

It is hard to end a discourse like this without one word of moralizing; and two things must be distinguished in all events like those we are commemorating,—the moral service of them on the one hand, and on the other the physical fortitude which they display. War has been much praised and celebrated among us of late as a school of manly virtue; but it is easy to exaggerate upon this point. Ages ago, war was the gory cradle of mankind, the grim-featured nurse that alone could train our savage progenitors into some semblance of social virtue, teach them to be faithful one to another, and force them to sink their selfishness in wider tribal ends. War still excels in this prerogative; and whether it be paid in years of service, in treasure, or in life-blood, the war tax is still the only tax that men ungrudgingly will pay. How could it be otherwise, when the survivors of one successful massacre after another are the beings from whose loins we and all our contemporary races spring? Man is once for all a fighting animal; centuries of peaceful history could not breed the battle-instinct out of us; and our pugnacity is the virtue least in need of reinforcement by reflection, least in need of orator's or poet's help.

What we really need the poet's and orator's help to keep alive in us is not, then, the common and gregarious courage which Robert Shaw

---

*After the Civil War, the Atlantic Ocean submerged the land on which Fort Wagner had stood.

showed when he marched with you, men of the Seventh Regiment.* It is that more lonely courage which he showed when he dropped his warm commission in the glorious Second to head your dubious fortunes, negroes of the 54th. That lonely kind of valor (civic courage as we call it in peace times) is the kind of valor to which the monuments of nations should most of all be reared, for the survival of the fittest has not bred it into the bone of human beings as it has bred military valor; and of five hundred of us who could storm a battery side by side with others, perhaps not one would be found ready to risk his worldly fortunes all alone in resisting an enthroned abuse. The deadliest enemies of nations are not their foreign foes; they always dwell within their borders. And from these internal enemies civilization is always in need of being saved. The nation blest above all nations is she in whom the civic genius of the people does the saving day by day, by acts without external picturesqueness; by speaking, writing, voting reasonably; by smiting corruption swiftly; by good temper between parties; by the people knowing true men when they see them, and preferring them as leaders to rabid partisans or empty quacks. Such nations have no need of wars to save them. Their accounts with righteousness are always even; and God's judgments do not have to overtake them fitfully in bloody spasms and convulsions of the race.

The lesson that our war ought most of all to teach us is the lesson that evils must be checked in time, before they grow so great. The Almighty cannot love such long-postponed accounts, or such tremendous settlements. And surely He hates all settlements that do such quantities of incidental devils' work. Our present situation, with its rancors and delusions, what is it but the direct outcome of the added powers of government, the corruptions and inflations of the war? Every war leaves such miserable legacies, fatal seeds of future war and revolution, unless the civic virtues of the people save the State in time. . . .

The warfare is accomplished; the iniquity is pardoned. No future problem can be like that problem. No task laid on our children can compare in difficulty with the task with which their fathers had to deal. Yet as we face the future, tasks enough await us. The republic to which Robert Shaw and a quarter of a million like him were faithful unto death is no republic that can live at ease hereafter on the interest of what they have won. Democracy is still upon its trial. The civic genius of our people is its only bulwark, and neither laws nor monuments, neither battleships nor public libraries, nor great newspapers nor booming stocks; neither mechanical invention nor political adroitness, nor churches nor universities nor civil-service examinations can save us from degenera-

*Shaw enlisted at the outbreak of the war with the 7th New York Regiment.

tion if the inner mystery be lost. That mystery, at once the secret and the glory of our English-speaking race, consists in nothing but two common habits, two inveterate habits carried into public life,—habits so homely that they lend themselves to no rhetorical expression, yet habits more precious, perhaps, than any that the human race has gained. They can never be too often pointed out or praised. One of them is the habit of trained and disciplined good temper towards the opposite party when it fairly wins its innings; and the other, that of fierce and merciless resentment toward every man or set of men who overstep the lawful bounds of fairness or break the public peace.

O my countrymen, Southern and Northern, brothers hereafter, masters, slaves, and enemies no more, let us see to it that both of those heirlooms are preserved. So may our ransomed country, like the city of the promise, lie forever foursquare under Heaven, and the ways of all the nations be lit up by its light.

18

BOOKER T. WASHINGTON

Address at Dedication of the Shaw Memorial

May 31, 1897

Born into slavery in Virginia, Washington (1856–1915) was the most famous African American in the country at the time of the Shaw Memorial dedication. Head of the Tuskegee Institute in Tuskegee, Alabama, since 1881, he had reached his peak period of influence with his address in September 1895 at the Cotton States and International Exposition. His declaration that "in all things that are purely social we can be as separate as the fingers, yet one as the hand in all things essential to mutual progress" opened itself to a variety of interpretations, including an acceptance of segregation. But Washington had criticized the Supreme Court ruling in *Plessy v. Ferguson* (1896), observing that the endorsement of racial segregation was related to the expansion of disfranchisement and lynching. How did he use the

From *The Monument to Robert Gould Shaw: Its Inception, Completion and Unveiling, 1865–1897* (Boston: Houghton Mifflin and Company, 1897), 91–95.

opportunity presented by the Shaw Memorial dedication to elaborate on his view of race relations?

An occasion like this is too great, too sacred, for mere individual eulogy. The individual is the instrument, national virtue the end. That which was three hundred years being woven into the warp and woof of our democratic institutions could not be effaced by a single battle, as magnificent as was that battle; that which for three centuries had bound master and slave, yea, North and South, to a body of death, could not be blotted out by four years of war, could not be atoned for by shot and sword, nor by blood and tears.

... There is a higher and deeper sense in which both races must be free than that represented by the bill of sale. The black man who cannot let love and sympathy go out to the white man is but half free. The white man who would close the shop or factory against a black man seeking an opportunity to earn an honest living is but half free. The white man who retards his own development by opposing a black man is but half free. The full measure of the fruit of Fort Wagner and all that this monument stands for will not be realized until every man covered by a black skin shall, by patience and natural effort, grow to that height in industry, property, intelligence, and moral responsibility, where no man in all our land shall be tempted to degrade himself by withholding from his black brother any opportunity which he himself would possess.

Until that time comes, this monument will stand for effort, not victory complete. What these heroic souls of the 54th Regiment began, we must complete. It must be completed not in malice, nor narrowness, nor artificial progress, nor in efforts at mere temporary political gain, nor in abuse of another section or race. Standing as I do to-day in the home of Garrison and Phillips and Sumner, my heart goes out to those who wore the gray as well as to those clothed in blue, to those who returned defeated to destitute homes, to face blasted hopes and shattered political and industrial system. To them there can be no prouder reward for defeat than by a supreme effort to place the negro on that footing where he will add material, intellectual, and civil strength to every department of state.

This work must be completed in public school, industrial school, and college. The most of it must be completed in the effort of the negro himself; in his effort to withstand temptation, to economize, to exercise thrift, to disregard the superficial for the real, the shadow for the substance, to be great and yet small; in his effort to be patient in the laying of a firm foundation, to so grow in skill and knowledge that he shall place his services in demand by reason of his intrinsic and superior worth. This, this is the key that unlocks every door of opportunity, and all others fail. In this battle of peace, the rich and poor, the black and white may have a part. . . .

REFRACTED REMEMBRANCE

Commemoration of the 54th Massachusetts after 1897 inevitably looked back through Saint-Gaudens's masterpiece. In the days after its unveiling visitors crowded in front of the work and decorated it with wreaths, although a Boston newspaper acknowledged that "people are asking, 'Do you think all this would have been done if Robert Gould Shaw had not been a swell?'"[17] Art critics praised Saint-Gaudens's work enthusiastically while sometimes finding opposite meanings in it. One critic described the monument as an image of racial subordination:

> He portrays the humble soldiers with varying characteristics of pathetic devotion, and from the halting uniformity of their movement, even from the uncouthness of their ill-fitting uniforms . . . secures an impressiveness of decorative composition, distinguished by virile contrasts and repetitions of line and by vigorous handsomeness of light and shade. Mingled with our enjoyment of these qualities is the emotion aroused by the intent and steadfast onward movement of the troops, whose doglike trustfulness is contrasted with the serene elevation of their white leader.[18]

Freeman Henry Morris Murray, the son of an infantryman in the 54th Massachusetts who was wounded at Fort Wagner, saw an entirely different vision of race relations in his *Emancipation and the Freed in American Sculpture* (1916). To him, Saint-Gaudens had depicted a patriotism shared by blacks and whites that "will tower above the odious 'color line.'"[19]

Dedications of public monuments often prompted the writing of commemorative poetry, but the Shaw Memorial raised this genre to a new level in American literature. William Vaughn Moody's "An Ode in Time of Hesitation," published in the *Atlantic Monthly* in May 1900, used the monument to criticize American imperialism in the Philippines. The poet depicted Saint-Gaudens's work as a witness of the recovery of American virtue in the Civil War. Shaw "leads despisèd men, with just-unshackled feet, / Up the large ways where death and glory meet, / To show all peoples that our shame is done, / That once more we are clean and spirit-whole." The betrayal of that redemption in the current "scramble in the market-place of war" was enough to "make his cheek / Flush from the bronze, and his dead throat to speak." Paul Laurence Dunbar followed a few months later in the *Atlantic* with his "Robert Gould Shaw" (Document 19), which responded to Moody and more broadly to the dedication of the Shaw Memorial. Dunbar's reminder of the white oppression of the 1890s— marked by the disfranchisement of southern blacks, the spread of segregation, and the rise in lynchings and other racial violence—indicated that the moral achievement celebrated by the monument was too hollow to sustain Moody's attempt to "remember now / My country's goodliness."

Debate over the resonance of the Shaw Memorial continued in several major works in the twentieth century. Charles Ives's "The St. Gaudens' in Boston Common (Colonel Robert Gould Shaw and His Colored Regiment)," one of the orchestral miniatures in his *Three Places in New England,* identified it as a cardinal point in his experience of his home region. An original poem accompanying the musical composition described the bronze soldiers as "Moving,—Marching— Faces of Souls! / Marked with generations of pain, / Part-freers of a Destiny / Slowly, restlessly—swaying us on with you / Towards other Freedom!" Ives's transcendental lyricism contrasted sharply with John Berryman's poem "Boston Common: A Meditation upon the Hero" (1942), which centered on a homeless antihero sleeping on a cold February night beneath the Shaw Memorial, which Berryman called a "Dramatic bivouac for the casual man!" Framed as a reply to William James's dedication speech, the poem argued that world war of mechanized mass destruction had rendered bankrupt James's tribute to individual will and moral courage. Berryman could only hope that "the casual man, the possible hero" would "rise / Homeless, alone, and be the kicking working one." Robert Lowell continued the examination of heroism in the modern age in his "For the Union Dead" (Document 20).

While the poets differed on the continued vitality of the Shaw Memorial as a site of memory, a group of African American and white Bostonians sought to renew its significance in 1981 after the city experienced a bitter struggle over court-ordered busing to desegregate public schools. The project restored Saint-Gaudens's bronze, which had deteriorated badly, and added to the inscriptions on the reverse side the names of the enlisted men killed in action during the war.[20]

The Shaw Memorial was also a starting point for the making of the film *Glory* (1989), the most widely discussed Civil War movie since *Gone With the Wind*. The producer of the film later said that he had been inspired to take up the subject when he walked past the Shaw Memorial on a trip to Boston. Other sources indicate that the project was launched by Lincoln Kirstein, who had published *Lay this Laurel* (1973), a stylish album of photographs and texts honoring the regiment and the monument.[21] *Glory* sparked debate for several reasons. It told the story of the 54th Massachusetts primarily from the perspective of Shaw, presenting him not as a capable officer who thrived in the army but as a confused young man who became effective only by rejecting standard methods of military discipline that closely resembled the control structures of slavery. In the key sequence, Shaw made the transition from bewilderment to leadership by recoiling from his mistake in following army regulations that required the whipping of an ex-slave in the regiment who had been absent without leave. In fact, army regulations prohibited such punishment, and viewers debated whether a cinematic truth justified the departure from historical accuracy.

The representation of African American soldiers in *Glory* also stirred controversy. Like the Shaw Memorial, the film did not portray African Americans who had served in the regiment, such as Lewis Douglass and William Carney. Instead, it highlighted the experiences of four fictional soldiers who supposedly represented different social types. Three of the four men were former slaves, which approximated the proportion of ex-slaves among African American soldiers in the Union Army but not in the 54th Massachusetts, in which three-fourths of the enlisted men were born in free states. Similarly, the emphasis on ex-slaves rather than the free black community of the North led to the deletion of a filmed scene of Frederick Douglass delivering a recruitment speech. Debates over such decisions demonstrated the strong public interest in the movie. Author Peter Burchard reported that his *One Gallant Rush: Robert Gould Shaw and His Brave Black*

Regiment (1965) sold fewer than 5,000 copies in the twenty-five years after its release but more than 50,000 copies after its republication with a still photograph from *Glory* on the cover.[22]

Glory contributed significantly to the expanded presence of the African American Civil War soldier on the American commemorative landscape in the 1990s. The National Park Service facility at the site of Saint-Gaudens's studio in Cornish, New Hampshire, raised funds for a new bronze casting of the Shaw Memorial upon its centennial in 1997 and sent Saint-Gaudens's gilded plaster version of the sculpture to the National Gallery of Art for long-term display. Several towns commissioned new treatments of the theme, of which the most ambitious was the African American Civil War Memorial and Museum in the Shaw neighborhood of Washington, D.C., a project launched in 1991. Seven years later, the city dedicated sculptor Ed Hamilton's *The Spirit of Freedom,* which invited comparison with the Shaw Memorial by presenting on the front side of a semicircular panel three African American soldiers and an African American sailor heading into war beneath a figure in low relief representing Freedom. The concave interior surface depicted an African American soldier taking leave of his family (Figure 4-5). A surrounding wall listed the names of all African Americans in the Union Army and Navy and the white officers who served with them.

Once again prominent in popular representations of the Civil War by the end of the twentieth century, the story of the 54th Massachusetts illustrated the cumulative nature of commemoration. A line of works in art and literature had done much to keep the narrative alive in American culture and had eventually helped it reach a wide audience. Each commemoration responded to the historical experience of the 54th Massachusetts and the current issues of the day, and each commemoration also reflected upon and drew energy from previous works of remembrance.

Figure 4-5. Ed Hamilton, *African American Civil War Memorial* (*The Spirit of Freedom*), **Washington, D.C., 1992– 1998.** How would you compare the ideas expressed in this monument with those of the Shaw Memorial?

Photos courtesy of Peter Kuzminski.

19

PAUL LAURENCE DUNBAR

Robert Gould Shaw

1900

Dunbar (1872–1906), whose father was a soldier in the 55th Massachusetts Infantry Regiment (created when the 54th Massachusetts filled up), wrote several works about African American Civil War soldiers. Such poems as "The Colored Soldiers" condemned the deepening subjugation of African Americans and asked, "They were comrades then and brothers/Are they more or less to-day?" How does his view of Shaw compare with the addresses delivered by William James and Booker T. Washington?

Why was it that the thunder voice of Fate
Should call thee, studious, from the classic groves,
Where calm-eyed Pallas with still footstep roves,
And charge thee seek the turmoil of the state?
What bade thee hear the voice and rise elate,
Leave home and kindred and thy spicy loaves,
To lead th'unlettered and despisèd droves
To manhood's home and thunder at the gate?

Far better the slow blaze of Learning's light,
The cool and quiet of her dearer fane,
Than this hot terror of a hopeless fight,
This cold endurance of the final pain;
Since thou and those who with thee died for right
Have died, the Present teaches, but in vain!

Atlantic Monthly 86 (October 1900): 488.

20

ROBERT LOWELL

For the Union Dead

1959

A great-grandnephew of Robert Gould Shaw, Lowell (1917–1977) was thoroughly versed in commemorations of the 54th Massachusetts and keenly aware of the ways in which he and Shaw differed. Lowell had spent five months in prison for his refusal to serve in World War II, in which he objected to Allied bombing of civilian populations, and he had been hospitalized repeatedly to treat manic depression. Lowell was also alert to the transformations of the city in which his family had long figured so prominently. He was in the process of resettling in New York when he presented his first version of this poem at the Boston Arts Festival in 1960. What meaning does Lowell attribute to the Shaw Memorial in the symbolic landscape of Boston? How does he connect the 54th Massachusetts to the civil rights movement of his time and to warfare in the post-Hiroshima era?

*Relinquunt Omnia Servare Rem Publicam.**

The old South Boston Aquarium stands
in a Sahara of snow now. Its broken windows are boarded.
The bronze weathervane cod has lost half its scales.
The airy tanks are dry.

Once my nose crawled like a snail on the glass;
my hand tingled
to burst the bubbles
drifting from the noses of the cowed, compliant fish.

*They gave all to serve the republic—a pluralization of the Society of Cincinnati motto inscribed on Saint-Gaudens's panel.

My hand draws back. I often sigh still
for the dark downward and vegetating kingdom
of the fish and reptile. One morning last March,
I pressed against the new barbed and galvanized

fence on the Boston Common. Behind their cage,
yellow dinosaur steamshovels were grunting
as they cropped up tons of mush and grass
to gouge their underworld garage.

Parking spaces luxuriate like civic
sandpiles in the heart of Boston.
A girdle of orange, Puritan-pumpkin colored girders
braces the tingling Statehouse,

shaking over the excavations, as it faces Colonel Shaw
and his bell-cheeked Negro infantry
on St. Gaudens' shaking Civil War relief,
propped by a plank splint against the garage's earthquake.

Two months after marching through Boston,
half the regiment was dead;
at the dedication,
William James could almost hear the bronze Negroes breathe.

Their monument sticks like a fishbone
in the city's throat.
Its Colonel is as lean
as a compass-needle.

He has an angry wrenlike vigilance,
a greyhound's gentle tautness;
he seems to wince at pleasure,
and suffocate for privacy.

He is out of bounds now. He rejoices in man's lovely,
peculiar power to choose life and die—
when he leads his black soldiers to death,
he cannot bend his back.

On a thousand small town New England greens,
the old white churches hold their air
of sparse, sincere rebellion; frayed flags
quilt the graveyards of the Grand Army of the Republic.

The stone statues of the abstract Union Soldier
grow slimmer and younger each year—
wasp-waisted, they doze over muskets
and muse through their sideburns . . .

Shaw's father wanted no monument
except the ditch,
where his son's body was thrown
and lost with his "niggers."

The ditch is nearer.
There are no statues for the last war here;
on Boylston Street, a commercial photograph
shows Hiroshima boiling

over a Mosler Safe, the "Rock of Ages"
that survived the blast. Space is nearer.
When I crouch to my television set,
the drained faces of Negro school-children rise like balloons.

Colonel Shaw
is riding on his bubble,
he waits
for the blessèd break.

The Aquarium is gone. Everywhere,
giant finned cars nose forward like fish;
a savage servility
slides by on grease.

NOTES

[1]Russell Duncan, ed., *Blue-Eyed Child of Fortune: The Civil War Letters of Robert Gould Shaw* (Athens: University of Georgia Press, 1992), 39.
[2]Ibid., 52–53; Peter Burchard, *"We'll Stand by the Union": Robert Gould Shaw and the Black 54th Massachusetts Regiment* (New York, Facts on File, 1993), 88–95.
[3]*New York Daily Tribune,* September 5, 1865.
[4]*Memorial R.G.S.* (Cambridge, Mass.: University Press, 1864), 109.
[5]George Fredrickson, *The Inner Civil War: Northern Intellectuals and the Crisis of the Union* (reprint, Urbana: University of Illinois Press, 1993; first published 1965), 164–65.
[6]Bliss Perry, *Life and Letters of Henry Lee Higginson* (Boston: Atlantic Monthly Press, 1921), 535.

[7] Alice Fahs, *The Imagined Civil War: Popular Literature of the North and South, 1861–1865* (Chapel Hill: University of North Carolina Press, 2001), 169, 175.

[8] *Boston Daily Advertiser,* October 9, 1865.

[9] *Boston Daily Advertiser,* October 2, 1865; Homer Saint-Gaudens, ed., *The Reminiscences of Augustus Saint-Gaudens,* 2 vols. (New York: The Century Co., 1913), 1:332.

[10] Saint-Gaudens, *Reminiscences,* 1:333.

[11] Ibid., 1:344.

[12] Ibid., 2:120.

[13] Edward Atkinson to Henry Lee, December 3, 29, 1896, Lee Family Papers, Massachusetts Historical Society.

[14] Higginson to Atkinson, March 22, 1897, Lee Family Papers; Higginson, "Address Delivered in Sanders Theatre, Cambridge, by Major Henry Lee Higginson, May 30, 1897," in *The Monument to Robert Gould Shaw: Its Inception, Completion and Unveiling, 1865–1897* (Boston: Houghton, Mifflin and Company, 1897), 24, 25, 34.

[15] William James to Henry James, June 5, 1897, in *The Correspondence of William James,* edited by Ignas K. Skrupskelis and Elizabeth M. Berkeley (Charlottesville: University Press of Virginia, 1992), 3:9.

[16] Saint-Gaudens, *Reminiscences,* 2:83.

[17] *Boston Evening Transcript,* June 2, 1897.

[18] Charles Caffin, *American Masters of Sculpture* (Garden City, N.Y.: Doubleday, Page, and Company, 1903), 11.

[19] Albert Boime, *The Art of Exclusion: Representing Blacks in the Nineteenth Century* (Washington, D.C.: Smithsonian Institution Press, 1990), 205.

[20] Shaw's sister Josephine Shaw Lowell had urged the monument committee to list the names of the rank and file who died at Fort Wagner, but the committee declined. It did instruct Saint-Gaudens to carve wreaths on the rear panel with the names of two officers killed at Fort Wagner, which through misunderstanding resulted in wreaths for all five officers who died in battle during the war.

[21] Kirstein took his title from an Emily Dickinson poem: "Lay this Laurel on the One / Too intrinsic for Renown — / Laurel — veil your deathless tree — / Him you chasten, that is He!"

[22] Martin H. Blatt, "*Glory:* Hollywood History and Popular Culture," in *Hope and Glory: Essays on the Legacy of the 54th Massachusetts Regiment,* edited by Martin H. Blatt, Thomas J. Brown, and Donald Yacovone (Amherst: University of Massachusetts Press, 2001), 230.

5
Lincoln's Legacies

No figure holds a more prominent place in American memory than Abraham Lincoln. His face helped to shape the cartoon image of Uncle Sam and remains as familiar as the penny and the five-dollar bill. The Lincoln Memorial has at times been as powerful a national symbol as the United States Capitol that it is positioned to balance on the Mall in Washington, D.C. More than one hundred other public monuments, museums, and preserved or reconstructed historic sites around the country honor Lincoln. A leading scholar reported in 1989 that "there are said to be more works in English on Abraham Lincoln than any person except Jesus of Nazareth and William Shakespeare."[1]

As one of the principal icons of American identity, the image of Lincoln has framed a range of arguments about the character and direction of the country. He has served as the exemplar of the humble common man and the personification of the power and dignity of the state. Discussions of religion in American culture have often centered on his significance as a moral and spiritual leader unaffiliated with any church. His reputation is inseparably linked to the achievements and betrayals of the "new birth of freedom" he heralded at Gettysburg.

American memory of Lincoln has developed in several stages. Perceptions of him during his life were transformed and deepened in a phase of remembrance that extended from his death into the 1870s. After a period of relative stagnation, commemoration resumed with new vigor in the years around 1900 and accelerated at astonishing proportions for several decades, bringing new themes, new forms of memory, and new promoters of Lincoln's reputation to the fore. This pace subsided markedly after World War II, but remembrance of Lincoln still played a key role in some of the most striking constructions of American identity in the second half of the twentieth century.

Diminished but unsurpassed as a historical symbol, he offers a crucial test case for the continuing vitality of American memory.

EMANCIPATOR AND MARTYR

Lincoln developed a variety of favorable and unfavorable images in his years at the center of the dynamic political culture of mid-nineteenth-century United States. Supporters praised his integrity, judgment, compassion, humility, and appreciation for ordinary laboring Americans. Detractors, depending on their perspective, condemned him as a rudderless incompetent, a crude hick, a tyrant, and an advocate of racial amalgamation. Lincoln scholars debate the extent to which he actively managed his public image. Such a successful politician could not fail to see the value of cultivating allies in the press or the appeal of highlighting his early work as a rail-splitter rather than his more recent employment as a railroad attorney. It is less clear whether Lincoln's strategic instincts or his agreeable nature better explains the frequency with which he sat for photographs or his willingness to accommodate two artists who set up studios in the White House for several months apiece to paint pictures that were soon adapted into widely circulated prints.

Significantly, both of these works focused on the Emancipation Proclamation. After an initial flurry of prints produced for Lincoln's campaign and inauguration, military subjects dominated the visual marketplace until the Proclamation intensified interest in the president. One survey has counted twenty-six prints issued from 1863 to 1864 that reproduced the text of the Proclamation; many others represented the event without the text.[2] While Francis B. Carpenter was working in the White House on his monumental canvas *The First Reading of the Emancipation Proclamation of President Lincoln* (1864), Secretary of State William Henry Seward told Carpenter that the painting missed the greatest moment of the administration. Seward felt it should instead have depicted the Cabinet at the outset of the war, boldly exercising unprecedented executive powers like suspension of the writ of habeas corpus in order to save the Union. But the prevailing wartime view regarded emancipation, whether jubilantly or bitterly, as the defining step of Lincoln's presidency.

This viewpoint did not necessarily imply that Lincoln deserved the

primary honor for the destruction of slavery. To the contrary, commemorations of emancipation led by African Americans more often
credited the workings of "the design of the Architect of the universe,"
as minister James Lynch put it in a speech at Beaufort, South Carolina, on January 1, 1864.[3] Such ceremonies of thanksgiving and re-
dedication carried forward a tradition of celebrating freedom and
urging full abolition in July 14 commemorations of the 1808 prohibi-
tion of the Atlantic slave trade, July 5 commemorations of the 1827
completion of emancipation in New York, and especially, August 1
commemorations of the 1834 elimination of slavery in the West Indies.
Black Texans established their festival of freedom on "Juneteenth,"
the anniversary of the arrival in Galveston on June 19, 1865, of Union
soldiers bearing notice of the Confederate surrender and the end of
slavery. The remembrance of the reception rather than the issuance of
Lincoln's decree typified the enduring emphasis of emancipation
anniversaries on the experiences of slaves rather than the actions of
the government.

Two months before his Emancipation Proclamation took effect in
Texas, the death of Lincoln dramatically shifted his image. The first
assassination of a president, less than a week after Lee surrendered
his army at Appomattox, stunned the nation and provided a focal point
for expression of the sorrow, anger, pride, and other emotions accu-
mulated over the past four years. Orators throughout the North ana-
lyzed John Wilkes Booth's deed and eulogized the fallen leader. After
thousands viewed Lincoln lying in state in the White House and the
Capitol, his body retraced the route Lincoln had traveled from Springfield four years earlier. The two-week-long journey stopped in Baltimore, Harrisburg, Albany, Buffalo, Cleveland, Chicago, and other
major cities, each of which staged elaborate ceremonies. In Philadelphia a crowd estimated at 500,000 watched the procession of the
coffin to Independence Hall, where it was viewed by lines of mourners
stretching for three miles. Countless Americans turned out to see the
funeral train pass through small villages and towns; as it moved
through Centerville, Indiana, at 3:25 A.M., a crowd of 2,000 people
gathered by bonfires. One student of Lincoln commemoration has
called it "the grandest funeral spectacle in the history of the world,"
and another has written that it was "the most striking state ritual that
Americans had ever witnessed or would ever witness again."[4]

Remembrance of Lincoln in the aftermath of his assassination and the end of the war tied him more closely to narratives of American national identity. Few preachers failed to note that Lincoln had been shot on Good Friday and to stress in their Easter sermons the parallels between the Savior of the Union and the story of Christianity. Journalist Josiah Holland sold an estimated 80,000 copies of an 1866 biography that similarly portrayed Lincoln as "eminently a Christian President," inspired by the Bible, suffused with piety, upright in morals, and glorified by martyrdom.[5] Another significant combination appeared in numerous prints that for the first time featured Lincoln alongside George Washington, a pairing of very different men that made sense when Lincoln became a symbol of nationhood. It was also only after the assassination that printmakers began to depict Lincoln with his family, a widely marketed motif that appealed both to the sentiment surrounding death and to Lincoln's new position in representations of the nation.

Lincoln's developing image did not necessarily displace the earlier view that the Emancipation Proclamation was his most distinctive achievement. Of the nine Lincoln statues unveiled between 1866 and 1879 in San Francisco, New York City, Brooklyn, Philadelphia, Boston, Springfield, and Washington (where there were three), only one did not depict Lincoln issuing the Proclamation. Henry Kirke Brown, who designed the monuments in New York City and Brooklyn, explained that "in any view of the late rebellion, the Southern interest in human slavery was its foundation and its motive power, and in consequence, the destruction of that institution by the President's Proclamation was the final blow to it and the basis on which the war closed. It has therefore appeared to me proper to represent the late President unfolding the sublime purpose of Emancipation."[6]

The conjunction of emancipation and nationhood appeared in the designs adopted by the two major Lincoln commemorative organizations claiming to act on behalf of the entire country, both named the National Lincoln Monument Association. The group based in Springfield placed above Lincoln's tomb an imposing monument in which the president, carrying a scroll marked "Proclamation," stood above infantry, cavalry, artillery, and naval units (Figure 5-1). The group based in Washington failed to raise the very large sum required for its proposed monument, designed by Clark Mills (Figure 5-2). The composition

NATIONAL LINCOLN MONUMENT

SPRINGFIELD. 1869. ILLINOIS.

Figure 5-1. *Certificate of Contribution to Proposed National Lincoln Monument,* **Springfield, Illinois, 1869.** How would you compare the representations of Lincoln at his burial site and at the Lincoln Memorial?

Library of Congress.

Figure 5-2. Clark Mills, *Model for Proposed National Lincoln Monument,* **Washington, D.C., ca. 1868.** How does the signing of the Emancipation Proclamation at the top of this model relate to the other tiers of the work?

Library of Congress.

placed Lincoln on the top of a tiered monument, signing the Emancipation Proclamation. The next level featured portrait statues of civilian Union leaders such as Salmon P. Chase and Henry Ward Beecher. On the third level was a cycle of statues intended to depict the progress of African Americans from slaves to citizens. In Mills's original design, this sequence culminated with a freedman kneeling gratefully at the feet of an allegorical figure of Liberty; the managers of the project quickly substituted a standing statue of Frederick Douglass. The final level of the work was devoted to equestrian statues of Union commanders. Whether coherently or not, the unbuilt work linked the Proclamation to the world of politics, the experiences of freedom, and the triumph of the army.

The significance of the Proclamation for ex-slaves was the specific focus for the Freedmen's Memorial to Abraham Lincoln (Figure 5-3). Promoters of this project made much of its origin, shortly after Lincoln's assassination, in ex-slave Charlotte Scott's entrustment of her former master with a five-dollar donation toward a monument for Lincoln. The gift wound up in the custody of James Yeatman and William Greenleaf Eliot, leaders of the Western Sanitary Commission, who took charge of a campaign to raise funds for a tribute from freedpeople. Although prominent African Americans like Frederick Douglass and John Mercer Langston supported the undertaking, politically moderate white Republicans made the crucial decisions. Eliot and Yeatman first adopted a design by Harriet Hosmer that surrounded an effigy of Lincoln with four statues that depicted African Americans sequentially as a shackled slave, a field laborer, a contraband aiding Union forces, and an armed and uniformed soldier. Unable to raise sufficient funds to build this work, they offered it unsuccessfully for the Lincoln tomb in Springfield and then agreed to sponsor the emancipation cycle on Clark Mills's monument in Washington. With the collapse of that initiative, they turned to a design by Thomas Ball that featured a slave crouching before Lincoln in a pose inspired by ancient rituals for the freeing of slaves and recalling the famous abolitionist emblem of a kneeling slave appealing for recognition as "a man and a brother." Eliot and Yeatman expressed some apprehension that Ball's highly conventional composition was not entirely suitable. They instructed Ball to remove the liberty cap worn by his idealized crouching slave and to make the figure a portrait of an ex-slave named

Figure 5-3. Thomas Ball, *Freedmen's Memorial to Abraham Lincoln*, **Washington, D.C., ca. 1866–1876.** What aspects of this design commended it to the leaders of the project?
Library of Congress.

Archer Alexander, whom Eliot had helped to gain freedom in wartime Missouri. They also asked Ball to show the slave "helping to break the chain that had bound him," to which the sculptor responded by depicting the slave extending his straining right arm and clenching his fist.[7]

Located outside the main commemorative zone of Washington, the monument drew an impressive crowd of government officials to the dedication ceremonies on April 14, 1876, the eleventh anniversary of Lincoln's assassination. Despite Frederick Douglass's protest that the statue "showed the Negro on his knees when a more manly attitude would have been indicative of freedom," whites generally praised Ball's work, and it essentially exhausted the opportunity to embed an ideal of emancipation in the civic landscape by connecting it to remembrance of Lincoln.[8] Although African Americans would continue to recall the coming of freedom in a variety of observances, white tributes to Lincoln would devote much less attention to emancipation in the next phase of commemoration.

21

HENRY McNEAL TURNER

On the Anniversary of Emancipation

January 1, 1866

The free-born Turner (1834–1915) was a minister in the African Methodist Episcopal (AME) church at the outbreak of the war. Upon the organization of African American regiments, he volunteered as a chaplain, and he briefly remained in that position after the war to work with the Freedmen's Bureau in Georgia until the racial discrimination he encountered in the army caused him to resign his commission. He was active in Georgia politics during Reconstruction and an important organizer of the postwar AME church. How does this address, delivered in an observance held at Springfield Baptist Church in Augusta, Georgia, describe the coming of freedom? What does Turner expect to result from annual remembrance of this anniversary?

Edwin S. Redkey, ed., *Respect Black: The Writings and Speeches of Henry McNeal Turner* (New York: Arno Press and The New York Times, 1971), 5–12.

Associated with the first day of January are peculiar interests, which in their accommodation to the world of colored men, will hereafter enshrine it in their affections with a deathless sacredness, forever and ever. This day which hitherto separated so many families, and tear-wet so many faces; heaved so many hearts, and filled the air with so many groans and sighs; this of all others the most bitter day of the year to our poor miserable race,* shall henceforth and forever be filled with acclamations of the wildest joy, and expressions of ecstacy too numerous for angelic pens to note. Before this day, all other days will dwindle into insignificance with us, and the glory that shall environ it, will, compared with which, make hazy in appearance all other days, God's day excepted. It has been the custom of men in all ages to celebrate certain days in commemoration of certain achievements or national transactions. . . .

The Fourth of July—memorable in the history of our nation as the great day of independence to its countrymen—had no claims upon our sympathies. They made a flag and threw it to the heavens, and bid it float forever; but every star in it was against us; every stripe against us; the red, white and blue was against us; the nation's constitution was against us; yes! every State constitution; every State code; every decision from the supreme court down to the petty magistrate; and worse than all, every church was against us; prayer and preaching was against us—enough to make us fall out with God himself. And why was it? We had always been loyal. The first blood spilt in the revolution for the nation's freedom was that of Crispus Attucks, a full-blooded negro. A negro, then, was the pioneer of that liberty which the American people hold so dear. England tried all through the revolutionary war to make us traitors to our country, but failed; we stood firm then and are firm still. Was it then because we are not really human that we have not been recognized as a member of the nation's family? Are we not made as other men? Have we not all the bones, muscles, nerves, veins, organs and functions as other men have? Are there any differences in our women? *White men can answer that question better than us.*

And so far as intellect is concerned, are we not as susceptible of improvement as they are? Cannot we learn anything they can? If we cannot, why make it a crime to be found teaching a negro? For it was a penitentiary act in this State, though it was not unlawful to teach a horse to read and write. But the whites not only refused to learn us themselves, but refused to let us learn *at all* if they could prevent it; at least law was against it, which was argument enough. They seem to have forgotten that they were shutting up in darkness, by refusing intellectual

---

*Turner alludes to the practice of hiring out slaves in year-long contracts that took effect on January 1, which often divided families.

development, that immortal spirit, that undying principle, that spark of Deity which was created with exhaustless resources, with a mind, though minute at present, which will one day swallow down or comprehend the mysteries of the universe. . . . Had the white people treated slavery as a trust from God, it would never have ended in a terrible war. It would have gone on until it became a social burden. It would have passed away so imperceptibly that no one would have felt the shock; more like a weary man going to sleep. But the way it was treated, and the ends to which it was appropriated, was an insult to God. And nothing less than floods of his burning ire and the thunders of his scathing judgement, poured out upon the guilty heads of the violators of this law, and crimsoned acres of ground with the heart's gore of tens of thousands, could satisfy divine justice and make slavery despicable in the eyes of a country which had loved it so dearly and nurtured it so long. . . .

This is a day of special gratitude to Heaven for many blessings which followed the exit of slavery. . . .

22

FREDERICK DOUGLASS

The Freedmen's Monument to Abraham Lincoln

April 14, 1876

Douglass (1818–1895) had helped to raise funds for the Freedmen's Memorial, and he agreed to speak at its dedication despite the exclusion of African Americans from decision-making authority in the project and despite his disdain for the design selected. How does Douglass explain its significance? The address offered an opportunity to review Lincoln's legacy as the country headed toward an important, closely contested presidential election. What political strategy does Douglass follow in assessing Lincoln and reflecting on the achievements and limits of emancipation?

John W. Blassingame and John R. McKivigan, eds., *The Frederick Douglass Papers, Series One: Speeches, Debates, and Interviews,* 4 vols. (New Haven, Conn.: Yale University Press, 1979–1991), 4:427–40.

We stand to-day at the national centre to perform something like a national act, an act which is to go into history, and we are here where every pulsation of the national heart can be heard, felt and reciprocated. A thousand wires, fed with thought and winged with lightning, put us in instantaneous communication with the loyal and true men all over this country. Few facts could better illustrate the vast and wonderful change which has taken place in our condition as a people, than the fact of our assembling here for the purpose we have to-day. Harmless, beautiful, proper, and praiseworthy as this demonstration is, I cannot forget that no such demonstration would have been tolerated here twenty years ago. The spirit of slavery and barbarism, which lingers to blight and destroy in some dark and distant parts of our country, would have made our assembling here to-day the signal and excuse for opening upon us all the flood-gates of wrath and violence. That we are here in peace to-day is a compliment and credit to American civilization, and a prophecy of still greater national enlightenment and progress in the future. I refer to the past not in malice, for this is no day for malice, but simply to place more distinctly in front the gratifying and glorious change which has come both to our white fellow-citizens and ourselves, and to con-gratulate all upon the contrast between now and then, the new dispensa-tion of freedom with its thousand blessings to both races, and the old dispensation of slavery with its ten thousand evils to both races—white and black. . . .

Friends and fellow-citizens: The story of our presence here is soon and easily told. . . . We are here to express, as best we may, by appropri-ate forms and ceremonies, our grateful sense of the vast, high and pre-eminent services rendered to ourselves, to our race, to our country and to the whole world by Abraham Lincoln.

The sentiment that brings us here to-day is one of the noblest that can stir and thrill the human heart. It has crowned and made glorious the high places of all civilized nations, with the grandest and most enduring works of art, designed to illustrate the characters and perpetu-ate the memories of great public men. It is the sentiment which from year to year adorns with fragrant and beautiful flowers the graves of our loyal, brave, and patriotic soldiers who fell in defense of the Union and liberty. It is the sentiment of gratitude and appreciation, which often, in the presence of many who hear me, has filled yonder heights of Arling-ton with the eloquence of eulogy and the sublime enthusiasm of poetry and song; a sentiment which can never die while the Republic lives. For the first time in the history of our people, and in the history of the whole American people, we join in this high worship, and march con-spicuously in the line of this time-honored custom. First things are always interesting, and this is one of our first things. It is the first time that, in this form and manner, we have sought to do honor to an American great man, however deserving and illustrious. I commend the fact to notice; let it be told in every part of the Republic; let men of all parties and opinions hear it; let those who despise us, not less than those who respect us, know that now and here, in the spirit of liberty, loyalty, and gratitude, let it be known everywhere, and by everybody who takes an interest in human progress and in the amelioration of the condition of mankind, that in the presence and with the approval of the members of the American House of Representatives, reflecting the general sentiment of the country; that in the presence of that august body, the American Senate, representing the highest intelligence and the calmest judgment of the country; in the presence of the Supreme Court and Chief Justice of the United States, to whose decisions we all patriotically bow; in the presence and under the steady eye of the honored and trusted President of the United States, we, the colored people, newly emancipated and rejoicing in our blood-bought freedom, near the close of the first century in the life of this Republic, have now and here unveiled, set apart, and dedicated a monument of enduring granite and bronze, in every line, feature, and figure of which the men of this generation may read—and those of after-coming generations may read—something of the exalted character and great works of Abraham Lincoln, the first martyr President of the United States.

Fellow-citizens: In what we have said and done today, and in what we may say and do hereafter, we disclaim everything like arrogance and assumption. We claim for ourselves no superior devotion to the character, history and memory of the illustrious name whose monument we have here dedicated to-day. We fully comprehend the relation of Abraham Lincoln, both to ourselves and the white people of the United States. Truth is proper and beautiful at all times and in all places, and it is never more proper and beautiful in any case than when speaking of a great public man whose example is likely to be commended for honor and imitation long after his departure to the solemn shades, the silent continents of eternity. It must be admitted, truth compels me to admit even here in the presence of the monument we have erected to his memory, Abraham Lincoln was not, in the fullest sense of the word, either our man or our model. In his interests, in his associations, in his habits of thought, and in his prejudices, he was a white man. He was preeminently the white man's President, entirely devoted to the welfare of white men. He was ready and willing at any time during the first years of his administration to deny, postpone and sacrifice the rights of humanity in the colored people, to promote the welfare of the white people of his country. In all his education and feeling he was an American of the Americans.

He came into the Presidential chair upon one principle alone, namely, opposition to the extension of slavery. His arguments in furtherance of this policy had their motive and mainspring in his patriotic devotion to the interests of his own race. To protect, defend and perpetuate slavery in the States where it existed, Abraham Lincoln was not less ready than any other President to draw the sword of the nation. He was ready to execute all the supposed guarantees of the Constitution in favor of the slave system anywhere inside the Slave States. He was willing to pursue, recapture, and send back the fugitive slave to his master, and to suppress a slave uprising for liberty, though his guilty masters were already in arms against the Government. The race to which we belong were not the special object of his consideration. Knowing this, I concede to you, my white fellow-citizens, a pre-eminence in this worship at once full and supreme. First, midst and last you and yours were the object of his deepest affection and his most earnest solicitude. You are the children of Abraham Lincoln. We are at best only his step-children, children by adoption, children by forces of circumstances and necessity. To you it especially belongs to sound his praises, to preserve and perpetuate his memory, to multiply his statues, to hang his pictures high on your walls, and commend his example, for to you he was a great and glorious friend and benefactor. Instead of supplanting you at his altar, we would exhort you to build high his monuments; let them be of the most costly material, of the most cunning workmanship; let their forms be symmetrical, beautiful and perfect; let their bases be upon solid rocks, and their summits lean against the unchanging blue overhanging sky, and let them endure forever! But while in the abundance of your wealth and in the fullness of your just and patriotic devotion you do all this, we entreat you to despise not the humble offering we this day unveil to view: for while Abraham Lincoln saved for you a country, he delivered us from a bondage, according to Jefferson, one hour of which was worse than the ages of the oppression your fathers rose in rebellion to oppose.

Fellow-citizens: Ours is no new-born zeal and devotion, a thing of the hour. The name of Abraham Lincoln was near and dear to our hearts in the darkest and most perilous hours of the Republic. We were no more ashamed of him when shrouded in clouds of darkness, of doubt and defeat than when crowned with victory, honor and glory. Our faith in him was often taxed and strained to the uttermost, but it never failed.... Despite the mist and haze that surrounded him; despite the tumult, the hurry, and confusion of the hour, we were able to take a comprehensive view of Abraham Lincoln, and to make reasonable allowance for the circumstances of his position. We saw him, measured him, and estimated him; not by stray utterances to injudicious and tedious delegations, who often tried his patience; not by isolated facts torn from their connection; not by any partial and imperfect glimpses, caught at inopportune moments; but by a broad survey, in the light of the stern logic of great events—and in view of that divinity which shapes our ends, rough hew them as we will,* we came to the conclusion that the hour and the man of our redemption had somehow met in the person of Abraham Lincoln. It mattered little to us what language he might employ on special occasions; it mattered little to us, when we fully knew him, whether he was swift or slow in his movements; it was enough for us that Abraham Lincoln was at the head of a great movement, and was in living and earnest sympathy with that movement; which, in the nature of things, must go on till slavery should be utterly and forever abolished in the United States. . . .

I have said that President Lincoln was a white man, and shared the prejudices common to his countrymen towards the colored race. Looking back to his times and to the condition of the country, this unfriendly feeling on his part may safely be set down as one element of his wonderful success in organizing the loyal American people for the tremendous conflict before them, and bringing them safely through that conflict. His great mission was to accomplish two things; first, to save his country from dismemberment and ruin; and second, to free his country from the great crime of slavery. To do one or the other, or both, he must have the earnest sympathy and the powerful co-operation of his loyal fellow-countrymen. Without this primary and essential condition to success, his efforts must have been vain and utterly fruitless. Had he put the abolition of slavery before the salvation of the Union, he would have inevitably driven from him a powerful class of the American people, and rendered resistance to rebellion impossible. Viewed from the genuine abolition ground, Mr. Lincoln seemed tardy, cold, dull, and indifferent: but measuring him by the sentiment of his country, a sentiment he was bound as a statesman to consult, he was swift, zealous, radical, and determined. Though Mr. Lincoln shared the prejudices of his white fellow-countrymen against the negro, it is hardly necessary to say that in his heart of hearts he loathed and hated slavery. He was willing while the South was loyal that it should have its pound of flesh, because he thought that it was so nominated in the bond, but further than this no earthly power could make him go. . . .

Fellow-citizens, I end as I began, with congratulations. We have done a good work for our race to-day. In doing honor to the memory of our friend and liberator, we have been doing highest honor to ourselves and those who come after us. We have been fastening ourselves to a name and fame imperishable and immortal. We have also been defending ourselves from a blighting slander. When now it shall be said that the colored man is soulless; that he has no appreciation of benefits or

*Lincoln and Douglass both liked to quote this passage from *Hamlet,* V, 2.

benefactors; when the foul reproach of ingratitude is hurled at us, and it is attempted to scourge us beyond the range of human brotherhood, we may calmly point to the monument we have this day erected to the memory of Abraham Lincoln.

DEMOCRATIC VISTAS

Commemoration of Lincoln waned after the outburst that followed his death. Except for a replica of the Freedmen's Memorial donated to Boston in 1879 and a statue funded by the bequest of a wealthy Chicago admirer in the 1880s, the eight statues commissioned in immediate response to Lincoln's assassination were the last such monuments to be dedicated until the 1890s. The pace of literary tributes also slowed, and biographers hoping to repeat Josiah Holland's commercial success were disappointed. Lincoln's former law partner William Herndon, seething at Holland's prettifications, made determined efforts to present Lincoln to the public as the product of a wide-open western society, more given to off-color jokes and erratic mood swings than Christian piety. But Ward Lamon's 1872 adaptation of this sensational theme sold fewer than 3,000 copies, and *Herndon's Lincoln: The True Story of a Great Life* (1889) also yielded little profit. Former White House secretaries John Nicolay and John Hay offered an entirely different portrait but experienced similar frustration. Their ten-volume *Abraham Lincoln: A History* (1890), the only work to draw on Lincoln's personal papers until the collection was reopened in 1947, described the president as a noble and sagacious leader. *Century* magazine paid a record sum for the rights to publish the book in serial form from 1886 until 1890. The magazine hoped to continue the spectacular success of its series of reminiscences on "Battles and Leaders of the Civil War" (1884–1887), but the inside account of the Lincoln administration lost readers for the journal.

Commemoration of Lincoln remained substantial even during this period of relative stagnation, and it began to grow rapidly again around the turn of the century. Ida Tarbell's *The Early Life of Abraham Lincoln* (1896), first published in *McClure's* from 1895 until 1896, was credited with bringing 100,000 new readers to the magazine.[9] Commemorations proliferated in the next decade. The founding of the Lincoln National Life Insurance Company in 1905 testified to the perceived appeal of the Lincoln name; it would soon be followed by the Lincoln Motor Company (1917) and Lincoln Logs (1918). Beginning in 1906, the popular *Collier's Weekly* led a highly publicized fund-raising campaign to preserve a log cabin purported to be Lincoln's birthplace in Hodgenville, Kentucky. The Lincoln centennial celebration of 1909 accelerated the commemorative momentum with countless observances. On Theodore Roosevelt's recommendation, the United States placed Lincoln's portrait on the penny. Roosevelt delivered the oration at the cornerstone-laying for a neoclassical memorial hall that would encase the Hodgenville log cabin in a temple-like setting. After the centennial, commemorative activity stabilized at a heightened level.

Several different themes, none of which carried forward the early focus on the Emancipation Proclamation, shaped the revitalized remembrance of Lincoln. The resurgence drew upon the culture of sectional reconciliation, as admirers described Lincoln as the transcendent embodiment of national reunion. To be sure, vociferous critics like United Daughters of the Confederacy historian-general Mildred Lewis Rutherford and William and Mary College president Lyon Gardiner Tyler spoke for many white southerners who continued to insist that Lincoln had tricked the South into a war that he waged barbarously. But this viewpoint was in decline. Southern cities observed the Lincoln centennial, and southerners delivered numerous speeches in his honor. Orators and authors often stressed that Lincoln was essentially southern in character. Novelist Thomas Dixon pressed the racial element of this characterization most aggressively in *The Clansman* (1905), the basis for D. W. Griffith's film *The Birth of a Nation* (1915), and two later books, all of which portrayed Lincoln sympathetically as a white supremacist opposed by unscrupulous radical Republicans.

Another dynamic force in the Lincoln revival was the emphasis on frontier democracy brought to the fore by Ida Tarbell. William Herndon had also sought to present Lincoln as a distinctive product of the West, but in his account Lincoln had wrestled with the bleakness and isolation of his society before mastering those influences. Tarbell, writing around the same time that Frederick Jackson Turner published his famous essay on "The Significance of the Frontier in American

History," instead described the West as a wholesome and nurturing environment. The greatest popular success in this vein was Carl Sandburg's *Abraham Lincoln: The Prairie Years* (1926), a romantic epic of Lincoln as a representative of the land and the people. That perspective informed the two best-known film portraits of Lincoln. *Abe Lincoln in Illinois* (1940), an adaptation of Robert Sherwood's hit Broadway play, traced Lincoln from his early adulthood in New Salem, Illinois, through his departure for Washington from Springfield. John Ford's *Young Mr. Lincoln* (1939) depicted the future president as a compassionate and quick-thinking lawyer beginning a practice and a political career.

A third powerful line of commemoration celebrated Lincoln as a model of national leadership. Long an active sponsor of Lincoln commemoration, the Republican party sought to strengthen that historic association in the administrations of Theodore Roosevelt and William Howard Taft. But Democrat Woodrow Wilson also claimed Lincoln's mantle, and World War I furthered the identification of the two presidents. In the succeeding decades countless politicians approached a wide range of issues rhetorically by asking, "What would Lincoln do?" Senator George W. Norris stabbed at the cliché during the Great Depression by suggesting that "Lincoln would be just like me. He wouldn't know what the hell to do."[10] Franklin D. Roosevelt repeatedly pointed to his predecessor as authority for New Deal and World War II measures, with support from playwright-turned-presidential speechwriter Robert Sherwood.

Over time the office of the president rather than the Republican party became the chief institutional beneficiary of Lincoln's political prestige. In 1945 Harry Truman incorporated memory of Lincoln into the White House by creating the Lincoln bedroom. This room became one of the most revered parts of the executive residence, although Lincoln, like other nineteenth-century presidents, had used it as an office. He never slept in the bed that Truman placed in it, which Mary Todd Lincoln had purchased in her refurbishment of the mansion.

The images of Lincoln framed by sectional reconciliation, frontier democracy, and presidential leadership clashed in two major commemorative projects. The so-called McMillan Commission, a panel of design experts charged by the Senate in 1900 with development of a plan for the renovation of Washington, revived efforts to place a grand monument to Lincoln in the national capital. The commission recommended that Congress move the train station in front of the Capitol, fill the swamp to the west of the Washington Monument, and continue the monumental axis from the Capitol through the Washington Monument westward to a Lincoln Memorial that would anchor the expanded and redesigned National Mall. The new monument would stand across the Potomac River from Arlington National Cemetery, with which it would be connected by a Memorial Bridge symbolizing sectional reconciliation.[11]

Both the site and the design of the proposed Lincoln Memorial prompted vigorous discussion. The president's former secretary John Hay, who served as Secretary of State under McKinley and Theodore Roosevelt, thought the McMillan Plan for a monument set off on the Mall was appropriate because Lincoln "was one of the immortals. You must not approach too close to the immortals. His monument should stand alone . . . isolated, distinguished, and serene."[12] Critics charged that this conception reversed the significance of Lincoln, the common man. Many of them proposed to honor Lincoln not with a structure in the capital but with federal construction of a memorial road that would connect Washington with Gettysburg, which like the battlefield might be embellished with contributions from states and voluntary societies. The alternative owed some of its support to automobile manufacturers seeking to provide a stimulus to road construction, but advocates of the plan promoted it as a more democratic tribute than the Mall proposal.

Henry Bacon's design for the Lincoln Memorial attracted some of the same criticism as the proposed site. Frank Lloyd Wright and Louis Sullivan were among the commentators who deplored the reliance on classical models as a bankrupt, misleading representation of Lincoln and America. Bacon's defenders argued that his approach set Lincoln in a tradition of civilization that had shaped him and the nation. The work also faced challenges from within the framework of classicism. Contrary to the sketches that McMillan Commission member Charles McKim had left at his death, which envisioned the memorial as a statue in an open colonnade, Bacon called for placement of a statue in a closed building surrounded by a porch with thirty-six columns (equal to the number of states in the reunited nation at Lincoln's death) because "the power of impression by an object of reverence and honor is greatest when it is secluded and isolated."[13] During a one-on-one competition with fellow neoclassical architect John Russell Pope, Bacon widened his entrance to enable viewers to see the statue of Lincoln from the steps and to look out from the building onto the Washington Monument and the Capitol. The historian of the Lincoln Memorial has called the resulting design "a porous, indoor-outdoor structure, a formal analogue to democracy," although other observers have stressed that it remained less open than Pope's later design for the Jefferson Memorial.[14]

Daniel Chester French's colossal statue of Lincoln (Figure 5-4), placed at the back of a central room flanked by alcoves that display the texts of the Gettysburg Address and Second Inaugural Address, has also inspired contrary readings from viewers struck by the attempt to depict majestic power and those who have seen in the portrait a pensive and deeply feeling Lincoln. Neither the building nor the statue highlights the theme of emancipation. Art critic Royal Cortissoz, who wrote the inscription above the statue, told his friend Bacon, "By emphasizing his saving the union you appeal to both sections. By saying nothing about slavery you avoid the rubbing of old sores."[15]

The other major commemorative controversy arose after advocates of Anglo-American friendship proposed in 1913 to place in London a copy of Augustus Saint-Gaudens's statue of Lincoln standing (Figure 5-5). No sponsors stepped forward to assume the costs of the initiative before the outbreak of World War I pushed it aside, but as the United States moved toward war in 1917, former president William Howard Taft's half-brother offered to donate a copy of a Lincoln statue by George Grey Barnard that he had commissioned for Cincinnati (Figure 5-6). The proposal prompted an uproar over Barnard's image of democracy. The New York Times argued that this Lincoln looked like "a long-suffering peasant, crushed by adversity" and suggested that "if that weird and deformed figure really represents the results of democracy, we can hardly expect Europe to fight that democracy may be made safe." Barnard's supporters asked in reply, "Are we ashamed of Our Commoner, so that we want to hide his hands and feet and gaunt figure from British eyes?"[16]

Barnard's most vehement critics included arts organizations closely tied to social elites, and his defenders claimed that he had depicted the ordinary American, but the dispute over democracy was more

Figure 5-4. Daniel Chester French, *Lincoln, Lincoln Memorial, Washington, D.C., 1915–1922.* What has been the effect of the decision to anchor the National Mall with a Lincoln Memorial in the form of a neoclassical temple housing a colossal seated statue?

Library of Congress.

Figure 5-5 *(left).* Augustus Saint-Gaudens and Stanford White, *Lincoln Monument (Standing Lincoln),* Chicago, **1884–1887.** What traits of Lincoln did Saint-Gaudens suggest in this portrait?

Library of Congress.

Figure 5-6 *(right).* **George Grey Barnard,** *Abraham Lincoln,* **1917.** Why did the proposal to place a copy of this statue in London cause so much controversy?

Courtesy of the University of South Carolina.

complex than these alignments and arguments suggest. Several polls indicated that an overwhelming majority of respondents preferred Saint-Gaudens's portrait to Barnard's more modernistic conception. The Saint-Gaudens replica was dedicated in Westminster in 1920, and the city of Manchester gratefully accepted the Barnard replica in recognition of working-class support for the Union despite the cotton famine of the Civil War. England, like the United States, would have multiple Lincolns in its commemorative landscape.

23

F. WELLINGTON RUCKSTULL

A Mistake in Bronze

June 1917

A prolific writer on art as well as a prominent sculptor, Ruckstull (1853–1942) was the most vociferous critic of George Grey Barnard's statue of Lincoln (Figure 5-6). His objections to the portrait included "the stooped shoulders; the abnormally long neck; the shirt collar sticking up like a rabbit's ear; the distorted clothing; the enormously exaggerated hands—held over his stomach as if he had the colic; the impossible trousers; [and] the gigantic and clodhopper feet."[17] For Ruckstull, these features departed from the photographic evidence of Lincoln's appearance and distorted the meaning of democracy. He recognized that Barnard illustrated some of the tendencies of modernism in art, and he insisted that the artist's obligation in a civic monument was not to express an original personal conception of the subject but to embody lofty community ideals in forms pleasing to the general public. What social and political views do Ruckstull's criticisms express?

> Because Lincoln was born in a log-cabin, split rails, built and pushed a flat-boat, was a Captain in the Black Hawk War and conformed to the indifference to dress which inevitably was forced upon the pioneers in

F. Wellington Ruckstull, "A Mistake in Bronze," *The Art World* (June 1917): 210–20.

every frontier region by the hardness of their life, he has been so often represented as a "slouch," as a "hobo-democrat" and as a despiser of elegant social forms, that it has found general credence among the unthinking—to the detriment of our country, because in this the auto-cratic reactionary forces of Europe have found one of their strongest points in their endeavor to show to what vulgarity our "slouch democ-racy" will reduce elegant Europe—if they go any further in the direc-tion of democracy. But this "slouchiness" of Lincoln is an absurd myth and a calumny, as we will prove.

We have many photographs to show that Lincoln always dressed in the best clothes his money could buy, whenever he could do so. He was even humanly vain, as every wise man is. We have the fullest record of this, for no president was ever more photographed, and he always had on his best clothes whenever he, deliberately, sat for his photograph. This dressing up to the best of his ability for public occasions proves, as well as does his political philosophy, that Lincoln was fully aware of the absolute importance of elegant social forms—if this nation is to realize its highest destiny.

Note the enormous and utterly untrue hands on Mr. Barnard's statue. One would say that the statue was intended only to show poster-ity what abnormal hands Lincoln had when in reality his hands were in proportion to his frame. They draw the attention so insistently in this statue that the head becomes of secondary importance, a violation of the fundamental law of all sane sculpture. . . .

Moreover, and most important of all, the face on the statue repre-sents Lincoln as if he had been a melancholy, distrust-inspiring weak-ling, which is utterly untrue. No man's face ever roused confidence more than the face of Lincoln. That is why he became President. Nor was he melancholy by nature. No national hero in history was so full of a sense of humor as Lincoln. He always saw the funny side of things, and most do have a funny side. Besides, his physical courage and moral courage were so great that he was the most serene man in the country during the Civil War. . . .

It is this serenity which invested him with that hypnotic power that conquered the confidence of the people and enabled him to guide the ship of state in his own way, and finally to lead the nation through doubt and fear to victory! . . .

Mr. Barnard says that in his profound travail to show "Lincoln's own self" he wandered far and drifted to Kentucky and, near the birthplace of Lincoln, found an old rail-splitter of the height of Lincoln and used him as a model to make this statue. Well, every rail-splitter is not a Lin-coln. There may be millions of rail-splitters, even of Lincoln's height, without having among them a man of such perfect *proportions* as were those of Lincoln. Lincoln's fine soul shaped his fine figure, grand head, and even the elegant small feet, which the photographs show. No other, no common man—above all a life-long rail-splitter—could serve as a model of Lincoln without being idealized in harmony with the photographs, and then the statue would not be literally true, and being not true would not be the "Lincoln's own self" which Mr. Barnard says he sought to render. . . .

24

GEORGE BERNARD SHAW

Comments on Lincoln Statue Controversy
January 11, 1918

The peaks of Lincoln commemoration after his assassination and in the first half of the twentieth century were international phenomena. In this letter to a leading collector of Lincolniana, the playwright George Bernard Shaw (1856–1950) examines the competing proposals for a London statue as an opportunity to consider the world significance of Lincoln and the self-representation of the United States. How would you compare his readings of the works to Ruckstull's interpretations?

The merits of the St Gaudens statue jump at the spectator at once. It is brilliantly clever typification, in the person of Lincoln, of the popular President, the successful politician, and the genial humorist. It is agreeably tailored, like a favorite actor on the first night of a fashionable comedy. It gives a good skin-deep reproduction of as much of Lincoln's face as most people saw in it after he had (rather unfortunately, as we think over here) grown a beard late in life. All this St Gaudens did; and I do not think it could have been better done. And if America is satisfied, the statue is in its right place—in America.

But in England the conditions are very different. The typical successful politician in England is not like the typical successful politician

Letter of George Bernard Shaw to Judd Stewart, January 11, 1918, typescript copy, Accession #80-2410, Abraham Lincoln Library and Museum, Lincoln Memorial University, Harrogate, Tennessee.

in America, and even less like Lincoln. Lincoln's humor does not touch us nowadays. . . . As to tailoring, our statesmen make a point of being the worst dressed men in the country: the St Gaudens suit of clothes, on which so much stress is laid on your side, would remind everybody here of Sir Charles Wyndham at his gayest on the stage.* In short, all the points you urge in favor of the St Gaudens statue would miss fire here.

But they would do worse: they would positively shock our English conception of Lincoln. For there is a cult of Lincoln in England, a cult which has received an impulse of late from Lord Charnwood's very penetrating biography. I can put our estimate of Lincoln in one word. Ridiculous as it may seem to those who see Lincoln as St Gaudens saw him, we perceive here that Lincoln was essentially a saint. That is the only interest he has for us or for any nation outside the United States. He was not our President, not our popular orator, not our humorist: he was a man of genius of the kind that crosses frontiers and takes its vessel far above and beyond the common political categories into the region which belongs, like the sky, to all mankind.

You may agree or not with this view of your greatest man; but I think that the moment you grasp it you will see that St Gaudens is impossible, and that Mr Barnard has somehow hit off the right conception for a statue of Lincoln for London. It is the image of a saint, and the head is not merely an aspect of Lincoln's popularity, but something like a mirror of Lincoln's soul. The statue is not faultless: what work of art is? As so much criticism of details has been published I may put myself in fashion by pointing out that though saints tread the earth lightly, and are generally alive to the tips of their toes, the lower half of the Barnard figure seems springless and dead, and the feet are feet of clay. Lincoln was rather given to dancing before the ark.† Mr Barnard has made a digression from the son of the morning to the son of the soil. There is, I think, a confusion of motive here: the feet are used to suggest that Lincoln trudged through ploughed-up fields as a boy, and the hands to shew that he wielded an axe and split logs. St Gaudens, in giving Lincoln a certain elegance for the sake of elegance, may have got nearer to the saint by accident than Mr Barnard has got as a doctrinaire. Also, in his reaction against the impossibly and inhumanly broad shoulders of St Gaudens, Mr. Barnard has swung over a little too much to the champagne bottle build. I make these cavils to show that Mr Barnard's deeper insight, and his escape from the clever superficiality of the St Gaudens or pre-Rodin phase of the art of sculpture, have not thrown

---

*Sir Charles Wyndham (1837–1919) was a British actor.
†This phrase alludes to King David dancing before the ark of Jehovah in 2 Samuel 6.

any dust in my eyes: I can see the worst of his work as clearly as the best. But I must give my verdict for Mr. Barnard. . . .

THE END OF AMERICAN MEMORY?

The enshrinement of Lincoln as an exemplar of American ideals had unforeseen consequences. Although seating was racially segregated at the dedication of the Lincoln Memorial on May 30, 1922, and President Warren Harding and Chief Justice William Howard Taft ignored the insistence of Tuskegee Institute president Robert Russa Moton that emancipation was Lincoln's greatest accomplishment, African Americans immediately recognized that the monument offered a valuable fulcrum in the struggle for racial justice. Gatherings began in August 1926 to meet at the Lincoln Memorial to call for civil rights. The political connotations of the site deepened when African American opera star Marian Anderson presented an electrifying concert to an integrated crowd of 75,000 and a national radio audience on Easter Sunday 1939 after the Daughters of the American Revolution had refused to allow the singer to perform in Constitution Hall. The Lincoln Memorial hosted more than one hundred large and small civil rights rallies over the next twenty-four years, culminating on August 28, 1963, with the March on Washington for Jobs and Freedom.

The March on Washington—highlighted by the "I Have a Dream" speech that Martin Luther King began by looking back "five score years ago" to situate the assembly in "the symbolic shadow" of Lincoln—dramatically elevated the prestige of the Mall as an American forum. The hundreds of rallies that followed at the Lincoln Memorial, focusing on a wide variety of issues and ranging across the political spectrum, did not always claim to carry forward the principles of Lincoln. But Lincoln offered an image of the democratic process enacted by the gatherings and of a national unity that transcended disagreement. Seeking to draw upon and strengthen that pattern of ritual reconciliation, Congress offered a location near the Lincoln Memorial, site of several important rallies against the Vietnam War, for the Vietnam Veterans Memorial authorized in 1980 to address one of the most divisive events in American history since the Civil War.

Important signs of erosion accompanied this expansion of Lincoln commemoration as a framework for American political culture. Maya Ying Lin's Vietnam Veterans Memorial (Figure 5-7) suggested an ambivalence toward the work that it replaced as the most visited monument in the capital after its dedication in 1982. The two glistening black marble walls of the Vietnam Veterans Memorial were oriented at a 125-degree angle to point toward the Lincoln Memorial and the Washington Monument "in apparent honor, yet accusation, too," in the words of one observer.[18] Similarly, African Americans recognized the limitations of Lincoln's racial views, as well as the strategic point that the icon of the Emancipator threatened to undermine the campaign for equality, and the civil rights movement largely abandoned him as a symbol after 1963. Thus, for example, the Million Man March of October 1995, one of the most massive attempts to update the March on Washington, pointedly reversed its predecessor by choosing the Capitol as its focal site.

Even before the wide-ranging cultural reassessments stimulated by the Vietnam War and the civil rights movement, criticism of Lincoln was becoming more commonplace outside of the South than it had been since the Civil War. In his influential book *The American Political Tradition* (1948), historian Richard Hofstadter profiled Lincoln as a "self-made myth" who demonstrated considerable political agility but little commitment to principle. A few years later literary critic Edmund Wilson published a provocative psychological sketch, subsequently included in his *Patriotic Gore* (1962), that depicted Lincoln longing for power from an early age and satisfying his ambitions with a dedication to the Union reminiscent of the nationalist zeal, and to some extent the dictatorial impulses, that Otto von Bismarck demonstrated in unifying Germany and Vladimir Lenin showed in forging the Soviet Union. These essays largely informed Gore Vidal's best-selling novel *Lincoln* (1984), which stressed the elusiveness and perhaps the emptiness of the core personality behind Lincoln's impressive shrewdness and literary flair.

Indifference to Lincoln probably grew faster than hostility to him. But his hold on the American imagination clearly slipped considerably during the last four decades of the twentieth century. Despite population increases and the expansion of tourism, the number of visitors to Lincoln's birthplace in Kentucky, the village where he spent his young

Figure 5-7.   Henry Bacon, *Lincoln Memorial,* **1911–1922, and Maya Ying Lin,** *Vietnam Veterans Memorial,* **Washington, D.C., 1981–1982.**
How do the Lincoln Memorial and the Vietnam Veterans Memorial compare in design, in theme, and in the experiences they offer visitors?
Photo courtesy of Christopher Thomas.

adulthood in New Salem, Illinois, and his home and tomb in Springfield all dropped sharply from the 1960s to the early 1990s. The number of articles about Lincoln in newspapers and general magazines plunged in the 1960s and settled after 1970 at the levels of the 1890s.[19]

Popular humor similarly indicated a decline in Lincoln's stature. The notion that Lincoln was too sacrosanct a subject for humor was once so strong that even Mark Twain deferred to it. Television comedian Johnny Carson helped to undermine this tradition in the 1960s and 1970s by frequently presenting skits in which he mocked himself for making futile efforts to find humor in Lincoln. Open parodies soon abounded. At the movies, the civic deity that a disillusioned new Congressman consulted for reassurance in the Lincoln Memorial in *Mr. Smith Goes to Washington* (1939) became one of the historical icons lampooned in *Bill and Ted's Excellent Adventure* (1989).

Survey data from the 1960s into the 1990s suggested that John F.

Kennedy absorbed some of Lincoln's popularity after the 1963 assassination that evoked so many comparisons to the events of 1865, including such official allusions as the solemn funeral procession bearing Kennedy's coffin on the ornate platform used for Lincoln. Particularly striking, however, was a 1994 poll that asked respondents to name a figure from the past who had particularly affected them. Among white respondents, Kennedy received the most votes of any historical figure and Lincoln received the second-most, but together they only accounted for 10 percent of all responses, less than one-fifth the number who chose a parent, grandparent, friend, or teacher. African Americans much more frequently identified a historical figure, most often Martin Luther King Jr. A designer of the survey concluded that "white Americans simply do not have a shared, revered public figure" comparable to King.[20]

At the same time, considerable evidence suggested that Lincoln maintained unique importance in American memory. A steady stream of books continued to celebrate him. Such favorable portraits as Ken Burns's 1990 television documentary series *The Civil War,* Garry Wills's study of *Lincoln at Gettysburg* (1992), and David Herbert Donald's biography *Lincoln* (1995) appealed to large audiences. The various Gallup Polls conducted between 1975 and 2000 to identify the greatest president in American history always ranked Lincoln first or second. Support for him was now divided less by region than by level of education, with respondents who had attended school for more years expressing more enthusiasm for Lincoln.[21] He similarly received more than twice as many votes as the runner-up in a 1994 survey that asked professional historians to name the person in American history whom they most admired.[22] In 2000, Congress found the upcoming two hundredth anniversary of Lincoln's birth to be sufficiently significant to establish the United States Abraham Lincoln Bicentennial Commission, giving it nine years to prepare for the event.

To the extent that remembrance of Lincoln has faded without replacement by a substitute, that decline in commemoration raises questions about Lincoln's future significance in American culture and, more broadly, about the prospect of memory as a basis for national identity. The French intellectual Ernest Renan wrote in his famous 1882 essay "What Is a Nation?" that "a nation is a soul, a spiritual principle," comprised of "two things, which in truth are but one. . . . One lies in the possession in common of a rich legacy of memories; the other is present-day consent, the desire to live together, the will to perpetuate the value of the heritage."[23] Similar conceptions of nationhood played a crucial role in the making of the Civil War and then in making the Civil War a foundation of American identity. Contemporary society and culture may not attach the same significance to shared memory or, perhaps, to nationhood. Whatever the future of the past, the best evidence of attitudes toward the continuity of the American experience is likely to be found in the mystic chords of memory emanating from the Civil War.

NOTES

[1] James M. McPherson, *Battle Cry of Freedom: The Civil War Era* (New York: Oxford University Press, 1988), 865.

[2] Harold Holzer, Gabor S. Boritt, and Mark E. Neely Jr., *The Lincoln Image: Abraham Lincoln and the Popular Print* (New York: Charles Scribner's Sons, 1984), 95.

[3] *First Anniversary of the Proclamation of Freedom in South Carolina, Held at Beaufort, S.C., January 1, 1864* (Free South Print, 1864).

[4] Merrill D. Peterson, *Lincoln in American Memory* (New York: Oxford University Press, 1994), 21; Barry Schwartz, *Abraham Lincoln and the Forge of National Memory* (Chicago: University of Chicago Press, 2000), 39.

[5] J. G. Holland, *Holland's Life of Abraham Lincoln* (Bison Books ed.; Lincoln: University of Nebraska Press, 1998), 542.

[6] F. Lauriston Bullard, *Lincoln in Marble and Bronze* (New Brunswick, N.J.: Rutgers University Press, 1952), 29.

[7] Kirk Savage, *Standing Soldiers, Kneeling Slaves: Race, War, and Monument in Nineteenth-Century America* (Princeton, N.J.: Princeton University Press, 1997), 114.

[8] John W. Blassingame and John R. McKivigan, eds., *The Frederick Douglass Papers, Series One: Speeches, Debates, and Interviews,* 4 vols. (New Haven, Conn.: Yale University Press, 1979–1991), 4:428.

[9] Schwartz, *Lincoln and the Forge of National Memory,* 160.

[10] Peterson, *Lincoln in American Memory,* 314.

[11] The choice of Lincoln for this place of honor was not inevitable. Architect Charles McKim, the most active member of the commission, urged at one point that the Lincoln Memorial should be at what became the site of the Jefferson Memorial, at the end of the axis extending from the White House through the Washington Monument. The anchor of the Mall and link to Arlington would instead be a grand triumphal arch honoring Grant. But plans for a Grant equestrian monument had advanced too far for full consideration of this alternative.

[12] Lewis Mumford may have had Hay's endorsement specifically in mind when he wrote, "Who lives in that shrine, I wonder—Lincoln, or the men who conceived it: the leader who beheld the mournful victory of the Civil War, or the generation that took pleasure in the mean triumph of the Spanish-American exploit, and placed the imperial standard in the Philippines and the Caribbean?" Christopher Thomas, *The Lincoln Memorial and American Life* (Princeton, N.J.: Princeton University Press, 2002), 41, 143.

[13] Ibid., 59 (quoting Bacon).

[14]Ibid., 91–92.

[15]Albert Boime, *The Unveiling of the National Icons: A Plea for Patriotic Iconoclasm in a Nationalist Era* (Cambridge, England: Cambridge University Press, 1998), 261.

[16]Schwartz, *Lincoln and the Forge of National Memory,* 273–74.

[17]"Mr. Barnard's 'Lincoln' Once More," *The Art World* 3 (October 1917): 11.

[18]Thomas, *The Lincoln Memorial and American Life,* 166.

[19]Barry Schwartz, "Postmodernity and Historical Reputation: Abraham Lincoln in Late-Twentieth-Century American Memory," *Social Forces* 77 (September 1998): 69–76.

[20]Ibid., 76–77; Roy Rosenzweig and David Thelen, *The Presence of the Past: Popular Uses of History in American Life* (New York: Columbia University Press, 1998), 127, 153 (quote).

[21]Schwartz, "Postmodernity and Historical Reputation," 69–70, 86–87; George Gallup Jr., *The Gallup Poll: Public Opinion 2000* (Wilmington, Del.: Scholarly Resources Inc., 2001), 58–59. In a 1991 Gallup Poll asking respondents to name America's three greatest presidents, Lincoln was included in 36 percent of responses from the South, 46 percent from the East, 49 percent from the Midwest, and 55 percent from the West. He was named by 19 percent of respondents who had not finished high school, 35 percent of those who completed their schooling by graduating from high school, and 57 percent of those with at least some college education.

White southerners who continued to harbor strong negative feelings toward Lincoln became particularly visible when the Richmond National Battlefield Park Civil War Visitor Center accepted the donation of a statue of Lincoln with his son Tad, which was unveiled on April 5, 2003, the anniversary of their visit to the fallen Confederate capital in 1865. Unanimously endorsed by the Richmond City Council (comprised of six African American and three white members), the statue was placed in front of a wall quoting Lincoln's commitment in his Second Inaugural Address "to bind up the nation's wounds." The Sons of Confederate Veterans led opposition to the initiative, arguing that imagery of national healing was inappropriate for a president who had unjustly invaded the South and waged war on women and children. One member of the Virginia House of Delegates said that placing the Lincoln statue at the Richmond visitor center at the Tredegar Iron Works, the manufacturing stronghold of the Confederacy, was "sort of like putting the Confederate flag at the Lincoln Memorial." *Washington Post,* January 9, 2003, B4.

[22]"A Statistical Summary of Survey Results," *Journal of American History* 81 (December 1994): 1210.

[23]Ernest Renan, "What Is a Nation?" in *Nation and Narration,* edited by Homi K. Bhabha (London: Routledge, 1990), 19.

A Chronology of Civil War Commemoration (1862–2003)

1862

July 17 Legislation establishes national military cemeteries for soldiers who die in service of country.

1863

November 19 Lincoln delivers Gettysburg Address.

1864

June 15 Union begins to bury dead on grounds of Robert E. Lee's forfeited home, Arlington.

1866

April 6 Grand Army of the Republic (GAR) founded in Decatur, Illinois.

1868

May 30 Commander-in-chief John A. Logan orders GAR posts to take charge of local Memorial Day ceremonies.

1872

Congress provides burial in national cemeteries for all indigent federal veterans honorably discharged.

1873

May 30 New York is first state to recognize Memorial Day as a legal holiday.

1875

October 26 Dedication of Stonewall Jackson monument in Richmond is first large-scale reunion of Confederate veterans.

1878

Chicago GAR introduces downtown Memorial Day parade.

1879

2nd Massachusetts veterans place first nonfunerary monument on Gettysburg battlefield.

1883

Women's Relief Corps founded.

1884

November Century launches three-year series on "Battles and Leaders of the Civil War."

1887

President Grover Cleveland draws criticism by proposing return of captured Confederate battle flags.

1889

June United Confederate Veterans founded in New Orleans.

1890

May 29 Dedication of Lee Monument in Richmond.

May 30 Memorial Day becomes a federal holiday.

August 18 Congress authorizes creation of Chickamauga and Chattanooga National Military Park, the first federal battlefield park.

1893

Confederate Veteran begins publication.

1894

September United Daughters of the Confederacy organized in Nashville.

1895

Mississippi adopts a state flag that incorporates the "Southern Cross" emblem.

May 30 Oliver Wendell Holmes Jr. delivers "The Soldier's Faith."

May 30 Monument dedicated in Oakwood Cemetery, Chicago, to Confederates who had died in Camp Douglas prison.

September 18–20   Dedication of Chickamauga and Chattanooga National Military Park.

1896

Sons of Confederate Veterans founded.

February 22   Confederate Museum opens at former executive mansion in Richmond.

1897

April 27   U. S. Grant's Tomb dedicated in New York City before a crowd of approximately one million people.

May 31   Shaw Memorial dedicated in Boston.

1905

Congress votes to return captured Confederate battle flags to southern states.

1906

Collier's Weekly launches fund-raising campaign for preservation of log cabin purported to be Lincoln's birthplace.

1912

South Carolina and Mississippi dedicate first state monuments to women of the Confederacy.

1913

October 22–31   National Emancipation Exposition in New York, featuring W. E. B. Du Bois's pageant "The Star of Ethiopia," highlights semicentennial commemorations of emancipation.

1915

March 3   Premiere of D. W. Griffith's film *Birth of a Nation*.

1922

May 30   Lincoln Memorial dedicated in Washington, D.C.

1925

March 4   Congress authorizes restoration of Arlington as memorial to Lee.

1926

Publication of Carl Sandburg's *Abraham Lincoln: The Prairie Years.*

1936

June 30 Publication of Margaret Mitchell's *Gone With the Wind.*

1939

December 15 World premiere in Atlanta of film version of *Gone With the Wind.*

1945

Harry Truman creates Lincoln bedroom in White House.

1956

Georgia adopts new state flag incorporating "Southern Cross" emblem.

1961

April Civil War centennial begins with controversy when a Charleston, South Carolina, hotel refuses to accommodate an African American member of the New Jersey delegation to the Civil War Centennial Commission.

1963

August 28 March on Washington converges at Lincoln Memorial.

1989

December 14 Release of film *Glory.*

1990

September Documentary television series *The Civil War,* produced by Ken Burns, attracts record audience for public television.

1998

July 1–3 Observance of the 135th anniversary of the battle of Gettysburg draws more than 20,000 reenactors and daily crowds of about 30,000 spectators.

July 18 African American Civil War Memorial dedicated in Washington.

2000

July   South Carolina removes Confederate battle flag placed atop state capitol in 1962.

2003

April 5   Richmond National Battlefield Park Civil War Visitor Center unveils the first public monument to Abraham Lincoln in the former Confederate states.

Questions for Consideration

1. What are the major eras of Civil War commemoration from the 1860s to the present? What transitions define these periods?

2. What patterns do you see in the social groups promoting various types of Civil War remembrance? Why did women take a more prominent role in southern than in northern commemoration?

3. Has Civil War commemoration merely reflected separately constituted social and political alignments, or has it shaped ideas and events?

4. Did the celebration of sectional reconciliation make the United States a more unified nation than it otherwise would have been? How would you measure national unity? To what extent did the culture of conciliation contribute to the deepening of white racism?

5. What opportunities has the culture of commemoration offered at various times to Americans seeking to build on the Civil War legacy of black freedom and citizenship? Have these opportunities been used as effectively as possible?

6. What characteristics of manhood has Civil War remembrance honored? What characteristics of womanhood has it honored?

7. How have Civil War commemorations represented the relationship between social classes in the United States?

8. How has Civil War commemoration related to religion? Has southern commemoration expressed a different religious imagination from northern commemoration?

9. How have the forms of Civil War commemoration related to its content? What accounts for the popularity of certain forms at certain times, such as monuments during the period 1865 to 1920 and historical reenacting more recently?

10. Is there a Civil War monument in your city or town? If so, how did it come to be placed? How has Memorial Day been observed in your town over the years?

11. What should be the policy of southern states toward public remembrance of their Confederate past?

12. Preparations are under way for observance of the bicentennial anniversary of Lincoln's birth in 2009 and the sesquicentennial of the Civil War beginning in 2011 until 2015. What events and initiatives should be included in these commemorations?

Selected Bibliography

Blatt, Martin H., Thomas J. Brown, and Donald Yacovone. *Hope and Glory: Essays on the Legacy of the 54th Massachusetts Regiment*. Amherst: University of Massachusetts Press, 2001.

Blight, David W. *Race and Reunion: The Civil War in American Memory*. Cambridge, Mass.: The Belknap Press of Harvard University Press, 2001.

Chadwick, Bruce. *The Reel Civil War: Mythmaking in American Film*. New York: Alfred A. Knopf, 2001.

Connelly, Thomas L. *The Marble Man: Robert E. Lee and His Image in American Society*. New York: Alfred A. Knopf, 1977.

Cook, Robert. "(Un)furl That Banner: The Response of White Southerners to the Civil War Centennial of 1961–1965." *Journal of Southern History* 68 (November 2002): 879–912.

Cullen, Jim, *The Civil War in Popular Culture: A Reusable Past*. Washington, D.C.: Smithsonian Institution Press, 1995.

Fahs, Alice. *The Imagined Civil War: Popular Literature of the North and South, 1861–1865*. Chapel Hill: University of North Carolina Press, 2001.

Foster, Gaines M. *Ghosts of the Confederacy: Defeat, the Lost Cause, and the Emergence of the New South*. Baton Rouge: Louisiana State University Press, 1987.

Gallagher, Gary W. *Lee and His Generals in War and Memory*. Baton Rouge: Louisiana State University Press, 1998.

Holzer, Harold, Gabor S. Boritt, and Mark E. Neely Jr., *The Lincoln Image: Abraham Lincoln and the Popular Print*. New York: Charles Scribner's Sons, 1984.

Horwitz, Tony. *Confederates in the Attic: Dispatches from the Unfinished Civil War*. New York: Pantheon Books, 1998.

Kachun, Mitch. *Festivals of Freedom: Memory and Meaning in African American Emancipation Celebrations, 1808–1915*. Amherst: University of Massachusetts Press, 2003.

McConnell, Stuart. *Glorious Contentment: The Grand Army of the Republic, 1865–1900*. Chapel Hill: University of North Carolina Press, 1992.

Neely, Mark E. Jr., Harold Holzer, and Gabor S. Boritt. *The Confederate Image: Prints of the Lost Cause.* Chapel Hill: University of North Carolina Press, 1987.

Sandage, Scott A. "Marble House Divided: The Lincoln Memorial, the Civil Rights Movement, and the Politics of Memory, 1939–1963." *Journal of American History* 80 (June 1993): 135–67.

Savage, Kirk. *Standing Soldiers, Kneeling Slaves: Race, War, and Monument in Nineteenth-Century America.* Princeton, N.J.: Princeton University Press, 1997.

Schwartz, Barry. *Abraham Lincoln and the Forge of National Memory.* Chicago: University of Chicago Press, 2000.

Silber, Nina. *The Romance of Reunion: Northerners and the South, 1865–1900.* Chapel Hill: University of North Carolina Press, 1993.

Thomas, Christopher A. *The Lincoln Memorial and American Life.* Princeton, N.J.: Princeton University Press, 2002.

Wilson, Charles Reagan. *Baptized in Blood: The Religion of the Lost Cause, 1865–1920.* Athens: University of Georgia Press, 1980.

Young, Elizabeth. *Disarming the Nation: Women's Writing and the American Civil War.* Chicago: University of Chicago Press, 1999.

ACKNOWLEDGMENTS

Document 1. Abraham Lincoln, *Gettysburg Address.* Reprinted from *Collected Works of Lincoln* (Rutgers University Press, 1953). Courtesy of the Abraham Lincoln Association.

Document 2. Woodrow Wilson, *Address at Gettysburg.* Arthur Link, ed., *The Papers of Woodrow Wilson,* Vol. 28; Copyright © 1978 by Princeton University Press. Reprinted by permission of Princeton University Press.

Document 6. NAACP, *Resolution on Confederate Battle Flag and Emblem,* 2001. The publisher wishes to thank the National Association for the Advancement of Colored People for authorizing the use of this work.

Document 7. Charley Reese, "Purge South of Its Symbols? You're barking Up Wrong Flagpole." King Features Syndicate. Reprinted with Special Permission of King Features Syndicate.

Document 20. Robert Lowell, "For the Union Dead." From *For the Union Dead* by Robert Lowell. Copyright © 1959 by Robert Lowell. Copyright renewed 1987 by Harriet Lowell, Caroline Lowell, and Sheridan Lowell. Reprinted by permission of Farrar, Straus, and Giroux, LLC.

Document 22. Frederick Douglass, *The Freedmen's Monument to Abraham Lincoln.* Reprinted from *Douglass Papers* (Yale University Press, 1979–1991). John W. Blassingame and John R. McKivigan, eds., *The Frederick Douglass Papers, Series One: Speeches, Debates, and Interviews* (New Haven, Conn.: Yale University Press, 1979–1991); 4:427–440.

Document 24. George Bernard Shaw, *Comments on Lincoln Statue Controversy.* Manuscript at Lincoln Memorial University. Reprinted from *Letters of George Bernard Shaw to Judd Stewart,* January 11, 1918, transcript copy, Accession #80-2410, with permission of Abraham Lincoln Library and Museum, Lincoln Memorial University, Harrogate, Tennessee.

Index

Abbey, Edwin, 47*n*
Abe Lincoln in Illinois, 6, 156
Abraham Lincoln: A History (Nicolay and Hay), 154
Abraham Lincoln: The Prairie Years (Sandburg), 156, 174
"Account of a Public Lecture" (Barton), 62–63
Adams, Charles Francis, Jr., 10, 100
"Shall Cromwell Have a Statue?" 105–8
"Address at Dedication of the Shaw Memorial" (Washington), 127–29
"Address at the Gettysburg Battlefield, An" (Wilson), 20–22
"Address on Dedication of Monument to Confederate Women" (Rose), 76–77
African American Civil War Memorial and Museum, 132, 133, 174
African Americans. *See also* race relations; slavery
  depicted on Freedmen's Memorial to Abraham Lincoln, 145–47
  depicted on Lincoln Monument design, 145
  discrimination against, 127, 174
  education of, 148–49
  enlistment of, 110
  film portrayal of, 131
  images of, as soldiers, 111–13
  Lee Monument and, 89–91, 99–100, 103–4
  Lincoln Memorial and, 165–66
  northern deference to Confederates and, 8–9
  rights of, 9
  soldier monuments, 26
  54th Massachusetts Volunteer Infantry Regiment, 109–37
African Methodist Episcopal (AME) Church, 147
Alabama state flag, 51
Alcott, Louisa May, 47*n,* 59, 111
Alexander, Archer, 146
allegorical statues, 27–28, 119–21
Allen, Otway S., 87
All Saints' Day, 42

Amateis, Louis, 69, 70, 74
American Political Tradition, The (Hofstadter), 166
American Red Cross, 61
American Revolution. *See* Revolutionary War commemoration
Anderson, Archer, 103
Anderson, Marian, 165
Andersonville prison cemetery, 62
Andrew, John A., 109, 116
Anglo-African, The, 114
Anthony, Susan B., 62*n,* 63
Antrim, N. H., 37
Arc de Triomphe, Paris, 33, 120, 121
Arkansas Monument to Confederate Women, 68
Arlington mansion (Lee home), 80, 93, 100, 171, 173
Arlington National Cemetery, 8, 38, 50, 80
  Confederate Monument, 23, 66, 67, 68–69, 91
Army Nurses Association, 60
Army Nurses Memorial, Massachusetts state house, 61
Army of Northern Virginia, 51
Ashby, Turner, 79
Ashe, Arthur, 104
Athens, Ala., monument, 39
Athens, Ga., monument, 38
Atkinson, Edward, 116, 120
Atlantic Monthly, 129, 130
Augusta, Georgia, monument, 38
Aztec Club, 15

Bacon, Henry, 157–58, 167
Ball, Thomas, 145
Baltimore, Maryland, Lee statue, 81
Barbara Freitchie (Fitch), 59
"Barbara Freitchie" (Whittier), 58
Barnard, George Grey, 158, 160–63, 164–65
Bartlett, Francis, 8
Barton, Clara, 60
  "Account of a Public Lecture," 62–63
battlefield parks, 16–22, 49–50
Battles and Leaders of the Civil War, 5